THE INFINITE CHARM OF FIREFLY GLOW

THE INFINITE CHARM OF FIREFLY GLOW

Lisa Shields

Iriswhite Publishing
North Carolina

The Infinite Charm Of Firefly Glow

Poetry copyright ©2005 by Lisa Shields.
Book cover copyright ©2005 by Iriswhite Publishing.
All rights reserved.

No part of this book may be reproduced or transmitted in any form or by any means, graphic, electronic, or mechanical, including photocopying, recording, taping, or by any information storage retrieval system, without express permission in writing from Iriswhite Publishing.

Iriswhite Publishing
North Carolina
www.iriswhite.com

ISBN: 0-9711072-6-2
Library of Congress Control Number: 2005921732

FIRST EDITION

This book is dedicated with love to Desiree Angelique Shields,

my daughter who taught me more than I dreamed possible

about love, determination and courage.

Saying Thank You

To my dad, Emil Thomas Golda. You never lived to see the cool stuff, Daddy. I miss you still.

To my dear friend, Windell (Tony) Spivey. You changed my life and my writing forever. *Semper Fi, Tony . . . always.*

To my sister, Christina Frohock, my number one fan and my friend. *With love from the Mooch.*

To my teachers: Stephen Anthony Rossi, for encouraging a brash kid to follow her dreams; Dr. Toni Libro, for making me write things I preferred not to; and Dr. Edward Wolfe, who always made me *wish* I could write something he would read out loud in class.

To my husband Charles. I could not be who I am now, had it not been for you.

To Craig Heddons, who said, "Lady, stop talking and START writing."

To my editors: Ralph Lock of London and *Oakhaven Manor*, a fine poetry website; and Jim Fowler, who never settled for less than my best.

To Ali, Ness, Jesse, Becca Savage Owens, Luke Owens, Kev Urenda, Pamela Bauman, Michael, and all my wonderful friends from the *Galadrial's Respite* website.

To Vinnie Demitus, his late mother Anna, Mary Shaefer, Cynthia Ammerman, Mara Broadaway, Sunny and Evan Greenberg.

To my beloved gang from the Twin Rivers Library. Rebecca, Sharon, Ina, and Nancy, I miss you all!

To Lyn and Jeff Van Riper, for the blessings.

To Charles Shields, and Ivy Irvane Spracklin, for the encouraging words and the awesome art.

To my mother, Loretta Golda. *No mom, I didn't forget.*

To Kirk Israel, of the *Blender of Love*, the first poetry website where my work found acceptance.

To Davena Aboiye, artist par excellance, (lately of Australia), and our mutual friend Ken from Bath. *I know, I owe you a sitting.*

To my collaboration partner Grey, of the West. *Who was that masked man?*

To Leon and Sondra Schlossberg, who read between the lines of my poetry and came to know me almost better than I know myself. Thanks for believing in me.

To the men and women who make the High Road School of Parlin, New Jersey, a positive and joyous experience for my daughter, Desi, and all the others in their care.

Special thanks to *Locks of Love,* the inspiration for my poem *Angel's Hair.* Locks of Love is a non-profit organization that provides wigs to children who have long term medical hair loss.

TABLE OF CONTENTS

Dedication v
Saying Thank You vii
Table of Contents ix
Publisher's Introduction xv

Wisteria Woman 3
Lover By Lightning 4
More Time To Think, Less To Dream 5
The Subtle Rainbow Of Your Touch 6
Day Star, Night Star 8
Maiden Soft 9
Eastern Longing, Western Dreams 10
Soul Connecting 11
All Kinds Of Quiet 12
The Infinite Charm Of Firefly Glow 12
Smoke And Mirrors 13
New Lamps For Old 15
Illuminata 15
Words Like Delicious 17
Infidel 18
Polite Conversation 19
The Gift Of Bittersweet 20
Intimate 20
Someone Else's Eyes 21
Tony Bennett And You 22
Not Quite No 22
Too Serious 23
Pay Attention 24
Other Colors 24
Far Afield Of Dreams 25
Mulled Music 26
Stealth 27
Truth To God 28
Sacred Dance 29
10,000 Miles 30
A Girl Like You 32

Contents

Not So Easily Broken 33
Speaking To The Sleeping Heart 34
When The Heart Decides 35
Plaster, Putty And Spackle 36
Sharing Water 39
Cedar Wood And Cinnabar 40
Soft Words On A Rainy Night 40
Reading Erotica Alone 41
Knowing 42
Pleasure Gardens Of The Gods 43
Tasting Breath 45
The Touch 46
Eventide 47
Old Seer In Tartarus 48
Questioning The Celestial 49
Plainer Words 50
Transubstantiation 51
Sirocco 52
Birth Of Self 53
Certain Knowledge 54
Candle To A Life 55
Healing Craft 56
Tremble 57
Dancing Lessons 58
White Marble Angels 59
Waiting Is 60
Battered Old Blues 61
Recognition 62
Fractured Self 63
Tussie-Mussie 64
Moon Dancing 65
Echoes Of Rain 66
Exigency 67
The Time Of Children 68
Shaman 69
The Scrying Bowl 70

Contents

Touch Of An Old Soul	71
Stone Flowers	72
Measure And Meaning	73
Atlas And The Nine Ton Stone	74
Mystic	76
Wood Smoke And Witchery	77
All The Clever Words	78
Stepping Away	79
10-Point System	81
Glints In The Mirror	81
Dignity, Honor & Grace	82
I Ain't Martha Stewart	85
Closure	85
The Elder Blossom's Request	87
Faulkner's Heat	88
Whisper Touching	89
Sourwood Hunger	91
Lattice Wings	92
Cold It Comes	92
Sleeping With You	93
Seeking Wisdom	94
Honors Rendered	95
Pop Rocks	96
Philadelphia, Art And The Kid	97
Better To Know	98
Not These Bones	98
Language Lessons	99
And I Do Fondly Love You	100
About You	101
Happy Father's Day	102
Mouth To A Kiss	102
Pleasures	103
Heart Of Mine	105
Eating Cherries	106
Rich Warm Broth	107
Miss Better Than Nothing	108

Contents

Hard Case	109
No Hearts, No Flowers	110
Klingon Love	111
When Charles Met Desiree	112
Sweet Tea Spring Infusion	113
Conversations With The Unconventionally Kindred	114
Gazing At Goya (One Part)	115
Moon Ridge	116
Feels Like Six	117
Midnight Shift, Angel Patrol	118
Aunt Anna's Kitchen	120
Soul Cocoa	121
Full Body Kissing	122
Consummation, Considered	123
A Time For Poetry	124
The Stars Above Me (9-11 Poem)	125
Talking To My Belly	126
Without A Word (9-11 Poem)	127
Soon	128
Want	129
Half A Loaf	130
In Your Dreams	130
Pale Shades Of Tears	131
What May Come Of You	132
Scattered	133
Decoration Day	134
Bitch On Wheels	135
Once Upon A Mickey D's Christmas	136
Heart Triage	138
Pickett's Field By Moonlight	139
From Where We Came	140
Reaching For Your Deep	140
A Bear For Yumi	141
Haiku For A Heart	142
Too Good At Goodbye	143
Adventures At The Green Grocer	144

Contents

The Daft Degree Of The Crocus	145
No Season Of Regret	145
Folding The Flag	146
The Show Of Hands	147
Grief	148
Magnolia Skin	149
King Stone	149
Seducing Onions	150
A Better Mousetrap	151
Angel's Hair	152
Pinked	153
Dark Mocha Man	154
Never An Angel	154
First Ghost	155
Pier Glass	156
Bunny Slippers	156
Not So Strong As That	157
Small Matter Of Translation	158
You Could Miss It	159
Inflection Of Silence	159
Momma And The Baby Buddha	160
Just Another Wave	161
Roots And Shoots	162
Rappin Rapunzel	163
Maybe Snow	164
Plan B	165
Got Wood?	166
Vernal	167
Tangible 24	167
The Heart Of Me	169
Crunching Numbers	170
Modern Day Lady Godiva	171
The Kids In The Back Row	172
Not My Buddha	173
Vintage	173
Brunch Date	174

Contents

Angel Born 176
Children's Hospital 178
Gazing At Goya (Another Part) 179
Midnight Embers 180
Reaching For White 181
The Man That Is, The Boy That Was 182
Simple Sipping 183
Writing Around The Cliché 184
Binaries 185
The Rules Of Riptide 185
This Woman 186
His Bohemian 187
Knowledge And Knowing 188

Autobiography 191

Introduction

In the 1997 movie *Contact*, Ellie Arroway (played by Jodie Foster) witnesses a celestial vision of incredible vastness and beauty. Emotionally overwhelmed by her inability to describe what she sees, Ellie can only say, "They should have sent a poet. So beautiful. So beautiful."

I had never before, nor have I since seen or heard such a warm, powerful and fitting tribute to poets and poetry.

We should pay more frequent attention to the poets we so desperately need. Why? Because poets have the courage to transcend societal conventions in order to translate our dreams, visions and emotions into metaphors we all can understand. Poets find ways to say those things we are too overwhelmed, shy, or ashamed to say. Poets are the mirror that reflects our lives and beliefs back at us for personal awakening and self-judgment.

The Infinite Charm Of Firefly Glow is the first published collection of poetry by Lisa Shields. Lisa has been writing poetry for more than 30 years. During that time she has personally experienced many of the ups and downs of life common to us all. Lisa's poetry evokes memories of those same experiences in our own lives, good or bad. Lisa suggests it is not too late to dust off forgotten dreams and renew the journey. She shows us that even in the worst of times, there exists an inner strength that pushes us ever onward.

There is more though, to Lisa's work than reminders and suggestions. Lisa exposes secrets; not only of her own life but ours as well. Lisa speaks to all the men throughout history who pondered the nature of women. Lisa speaks from the heart and soul of every woman. Lisa knows the truth, and tells.

In a recent letter to one of her friends, Lisa wrote, "Some people want to be stars; the brighter the better. But stars give no warmth, just an illusion of light. I would rather be the flash of a firefly you can catch with your hands, than the ancient light of a distant star no one can ever touch."

Lisa Shields is a bright flash indeed. She imparts warmth, humor, sadness, triumph and occasional naughtiness in simple terms that make us wonder why we never wrote those same words ourselves. Lisa's rarest quality is also her most endearing. She truly inspires many of her readers to want to write . . . poetry.

Doctor Arroway, they should have sent Lisa Shields.

Editor

The Infinite Charm of Firefly Glow

Wisteria Woman

Violet lavender drug
slipping beneath my skin,
shucking off the stale air
of too long shut in,
too long shut away,
whispering to me
to breathe deep and be.

The clothes fall away
till I stand like mother Eve,
two bites before the apple.
Lips blush to rose,
and the tongue tastes
of sweet, tart pomegranate,
while a wisp of wind
carries the hair to frame my face.

All I have been is pollen dusted,
the wisteria sweet
kissing deep,
till I feel the promise of fertile,
drooping fat on a vine,
petals that promise nothing,
but hint at all.

A month from honeysuckle still to come,
but I can taste the nights,
and raise my eyes to the mantle of sky,
suddenly clad in the skin
of every moonlit woman,
and beckoning with my being
for you to dance beneath
the far-flung sky
in the arms of a Wisteria Woman.

❧ Lover By Lightning

They say a storm in the desert
will make you believe
that God and nature
are close kin,
their wonders to behold.
Oh, I must be mad . . .
because the bolt and flash
just left the small hairs dancing
on the back of my neck
and I am not afraid.

Rather I would cast off my clothes
take your hand
and lead you to the mesa
where lightning falls like rain,
ask you to take my body,
take my soul
and defy God and nature
while the air dances
with electricity.

I taste copper on my tongue,
the dried salt on your skin
and the unleashed glory
in your eyes
as your hand spans my waist.
You pull me close
and kiss me, with white fire
falling all around.

The wind howls in rage
that we are foolish,
to dare love like this.
It tears at my hair
making me a fallen angel,
a crazed witch in your arms.

But the danger is nothing.
Every breath after the first
is a risk . . .
but to have you
to know you
I will risk all.
If we are consumed
on this desert night
then I will have had you
heart and soul
on the broad mesa,
dancing in your embrace
before the eyes of the gods.

◊ MORE TIME TO THINK, LESS TO DREAM

I wake to rain,
the same fat drops they pray for
in the wind-swept arroyo,
with the touch of your fingers
still lingering on my skin,
the soft ghost of your kiss
pressed against sleepy lips.
I know you watched again
as I lay sleeping,
chased the hair from my cheek,
and wondered what would become
of you,
of me,
of us,
if life had its usual
maddened *bull in a china shop*
way with our hearts.
Half mad with fear
seeing ghosts
in the dance of the curtains,
you are thinking it was simpler

when the amber glow
was something unknown.
You can never miss the color
you have not seen,
the touch your skin never knew.
Simpler when I was a dream
and you were the dreamer.
Now you peer into what may come
wonder
weigh
and ponder
if you want me to pay the price
of a love
that presses itself
from dream to real.
More time to think,
less to dream,
but the cost is counted, my love.
If never I hold the gleaming gem
softly in my hand
still I will pay
for wanting to make it mine, alone.
If my fingers shake,
and it slips through my hands
falling into the cascade basin,
still I will pay
whether it was mine forever to keep,
or just for one shining instant.

☙ THE SUBTLE RAINBOW OF YOUR TOUCH

Rational is good.
Logic soothing.
Yes, I need the cool comfort
of ordered thought
that allows me to sort
all these tangles of emotional thread.

I committed the crime
of letting my true face be seen,
telling myself you would not love
could not love
the gray eyes
and odd assortment of features.
It made hiding comfortable.

But my mask slipped.
You never said you could see me,
yet the whole time I sought
precious concealment,
you were looking in my eyes.
I thought I kept my heart well buried,
but instead it was nestled in your hands,
touched so lightly I felt no fear
because it was a touch I knew.
We spoke so lightly of longing,
in cool general terms.

It should have come as no shock
that when I turned
you were close enough for lips
to touch, to drag slowly along my shoulder
until I was so softly drugged
it did not occur
that somewhere love had made a quiet entrance.

Now the thought of you
suffuses this skin with a longing
that will not still the helium butterfly
that lights and floats,
clings to my ribs
and laughs when I tell myself
that I will not lose myself
in the rainbow regard of your spirit.

❧ Day Star, Night Star

When love was a Goddess,
they gave her two forms
because her brilliance was visible
twice in the sky of every year.

In the Month of May,
she rises before the dawn,
the last bright object shining
before the sun returns.

In the Month of October,
she is the midnight jewel,
crisp, clear and beckoning,
the sweet whisper of the unknown,
soft promises to be filled
beneath layers of darkness
and covers of down.

The daystar looks at love
with the calm acceptance of intellect,
seeing it plainly, without dancing shadows.

The night star sees something else,
in the quiet of a still night,
more akin to basic hunger than thought.

Between the two,
is the truth of Venus,
love without false hope and illusion,
but still the wonder of a child
for whom the dancing stars
are ever a delight.

Each holds in its heart
half of the knowing.
Day Star,
Night Star,
trying to piece together
the great puzzle of the Cosmos.

❧ Maiden Soft

Hair falling maiden soft
from the scatter of pins,
eyes that cannot meet yours,
though a moment ago
they were laughing.
Then that look took you,
and you reached out
loosened the hair
and caught your breath
when it fell like thin silk around me.
We are all decent,
and no
you have not even tasted
my breath
but I know if I look at you,
you will.
With cheeks
flushed with the flare
of unspoken heat,
and breathless knowledge
will you
would you
and you are so damned close
that surely you will feel the blush
would you
will you . . .
And before I can ask,
you bring your lips down
and they are as hot
as the color you gave my face
when my hair fell maiden soft
beneath your gentle
seeking fingers.

❧ Eastern Longing, Western Dreams

There is something about this
layered with the smoke
of a hundred joss sticks
lit to make happy
the household gods.

I smell jasmine and ginger
and imagine you
walking on the shore
of an impossibly blue ocean,
feel the breeze
touch your face
and hear your breath
slow and even
as the waves lick
softly at your feet.

I see myself
in a different world
where the sea is not gray,
and twin hearts are not parted.
Longing is not only a word.
Yearning is bone deep,
and cuts like crystal shards
glittering in the sun.

I see your eyes full on me,
lighting
consuming.
I do not need your touch
to feel possessed.

Heady stuff, these dreams
that carry me
on Pegasus' wings
and drop me
still drowsy
into your waiting arms.

✿ Soul Connecting

What was I doing there,
when you showed up, asking and offering nothing
till I intruded in your world
with the casual grace of a hurricane?
We decided to talk, and I found
safe haven I had no right to ask.

I was free to go, you were free to stay
and the touching was a different kind
that left me weak, and breathless.
I chose for us both,
with that first impertinent question,
and you allowed me in.

I had no right to offer my heart,
but the hunger was in you as well
and every choice since
has been a ricochet between soul and brain,
that I never asked the cost of . . .

until now.

Now I wonder what I have done to us both,
drawing you firmly in like that.
You say you cannot resist me,
and I cannot resist
what you offer to my spirit.

So I offer you the next move,
because I began this dance,
and will accept
what your soul will offer
to a she-devil
without sense,
manners or
the good taste to wait
until something is given with an open hand.

❧ All Kinds Of Quiet

Silence need not be a death knell;
need not be cold, or stifling.
There is the quiet
between lips about to kiss,
there is the moment
of fond memory
steeped in lavender,
the second when words fail,
and you wrap yourself
deeply around a heart.
Oh the quiet
of a ticking minute
when the tongue knows well
what it wishes to say,
the ears know better
what they wish to hear,
and quiet is full of something
unspoken
but completely understood
below the skin,
and above emotion.

❧ The Infinite Charm Of Firefly Glow

You are drawn
to the glimmer that flashes
not at midnight,
but at dusk
when the heart's eyes
are seeking some morsel of light,
and the stars are not yet ready to dance.

Light is warmth,
hope,
and perhaps the gift of a dream

bestowed by a still sleeping moon.
You seek the perfection of an orchid,
still drooping with the promise of rain,
and that shimmer in the dark
tastes like honeysuckle
on a tongue too long dry.

On a summer night,
when it is sticky, steamy and still,
I understand the urge
to fall in love with a firefly
when your heart needs
a simple flame to breathe.

☙ SMOKE AND MIRRORS

Candlelight
happy shadows dance across the skin
a soft sigh that is invitation
an embrace that is trust
all wound together
in a well-worn sheet.

It was all bait once; all enticement
without a clue of culmination.
But the game was such
that only acquisition counted.
Savoring was unknown;
it was everything you could grab
wow . . . great . . . forgot your name
I have this early meeting . . .
And whatever elation you might have gotten
from a hasty touch
or hurried performance
bled quickly from your soul
when you came to know
with iron-cold certainty

that you had been discarded . . .
more tissue than woman.

You forgot the insult
but remembered the lesson.
It took the gossamer from your wings
the joy from your step
until you had the message ground
into you with broken glass,
that your spirit was excess baggage.

So when someone looks in your eyes
years after you've given up on such games,
gives back kindness,
wraps you in warm regard,
and says you are rare,
beautiful,
and God yes, sexy,
you rock back on your heels
and say "No . . ."

Not because you don't wish
or because you don't hunger,
but because they never did kill
the spirit of *you*.
It burrowed deep . . . slept,
and it takes the right mix
to bring it back to where
the blood is in your ears,
blushes come naturally again
and you start to think
that maybe you always were quite splendid.

When the blood begins to sing,
races beneath your skin,
fills your breasts
with life and living
and the juices come like spring rain . . .
you start to wonder
if it is possible to savor something you never tasted.

❧ New Lamps For Old

Someone came up with the bright idea
to use old coffee, best drunk hot,
add some ice
and make something completely different.
Someone took the bagels
that were day-old stale,
sliced them and spiced them,
baked them *crunchy*,
and sold them for three times the price fresh.
Recycling they call it.
Well, I have this heart,
which has blown hot and cold,
and is downright crispy in places.
Maybe what I need
is not a new heart,
but a marketing genius
who can make what I have
seem like something someone needs;
something completely different . . .
but please guy,
no heart-on-a-stick.
I sort of like the holes
right where they are now.

❧ Illuminata

You bring calm and tranquility,
set my heart to glowing
with a few words,
the grace of your smile
gifting me gently,
lifting my spirit,
and this is becoming
my natural state,

who I am
and how I am . . .
Frantic,
restless,
harried . . .
are not even words to me.
You say this was all inside me,
that you had no part in this transfiguration,
but you would be wrong.
It began with your touch.
You took a wounded spirit
bathed it with love,
warmed it with gentle regard
and held it close and dear
until the shaking stopped,
until the urge to hurt myself
before someone else could
dissolved into a faint echo
and I began to hear
the glorious music
of my own heart
when it beat in countermeasure
to the soft sound of yours.
No wonder that the poets
have wriggled,
struggled
and sworn for centuries
to give voice to this state;
when a complete person
becomes somehow more complete,
when a heart knows its name,
its voice
and, yes my dear one,
its destiny
in the rainbow light
of all that you gave me
when you called me *love.*

❧ WORDS LIKE DELICIOUS

Not sporting,
no, not even one slice of fair
to say a word like that
when you're talking about *me*.

Delicious is something reserved
for that which beguiles the tongue,
seduces the senses,
and makes everything
seem to be rolled in caramel,
bathed in chocolate,
then left to set
while taste, touch and smell
clamor to defy
the very best of our intentions.

Delicious is something
we know darned well
will make us fat, jailed, or blushing
but we always find a way
to sneak a taste,
because tasting is not eating.

So you see,
I can't be . . . well, delicious
even if I *feel* that way
when you look at me
like something
you simply must have
this once.

❧ INFIDEL

You get past the first layers of human,
find the places where the chords
tremble at the same tone,
and finally say what we already knew.

Infidel.
"Birds of a feather..." too simply put.
We read the scarlet "A,"
know that the worst pain
is not in the *wrong* that we did,
but the price of making good.

Infidel.
Honor demands a return.
If the place is cold,
if the arms feel like sticks and bones,
and the heart cries for another,
we turn the bushido blade inward,
try to cut loose the longing.

Infidel.
You paid more than I,
because you actually tasted the bliss.
But I recognized the moment
when I knew all was lost,
when a *goodbye* was needed.
Yet I stayed
despite the sin of wanting.

Infidel.
Something akin to forgiveness
begins the day you stop saying
to that pale and pretty bygone dream,
I did not *mean* to love you
because all that matters
in your truest heart
is that one day, you did.

You return to the old haunts,
sleep on the sheets,
go through the motions,
but you paid the price of the infidel,
in the blood pennies of essence.

Now Cheron has carried you back
less the baggage of your heart.
Sleep is futile since you gave up on dreams,
and the small bit of comfort
is having done the right thing,
when all it cost
was all you ever were inside.

☙ Polite Conversation

When exchanging polite conversation,
it is perfectly rude
to point out that the lady
is hiding in her hair,
looking at anything but you,
when all you did
was look at her mouth,
as if a perfect ripe pear
that would take
only the lightest of pressure
to spill its sweetness
into your lips,
and tell you once again
that the proof of the pudding,
is in the tasting.
But in polite conversation,
there is no room
for a look like that,
and you damned well know it.

☙ THE GIFT OF BITTERSWEET

"What shall I get you," he asked,
not really thinking
as they walked the park path.
She did not pause,
did not even break stride.
"Bittersweet" she said,
"enough to make a wreath."
He could have gathered it
right then,
at a cost of only his time.
But instead he explained
why it was such a bad idea,
and quite a bit of trouble,
besides, what did she know
of making wreathes?
Then he walked calmly,
quite pleased to have laid the matter to rest,
but he did not see her face,
did not read her eyes
and never once did he ask himself
why after all those years
all she could think to ask of him
was a gift of bittersweet.

☙ INTIMATE

You've been trying to look in my eyes
since the first cheeky hello,
as if you wished to see something
I carefully concealed,
hidden in gray ashes,
sheltered from a world
that delights
in crushing butterflies

and charring moths,
an unhealthy place
for things with wings.

I have looked everywhere else,
and the only thing left
is to square my shoulders,
raise my chin,
and let you see
that there really is no secret,
only eyes like the Atlantic
just before a hurricane,
no force of nature,
just me.

ଓଃ Someone Else's Eyes

We never see ourselves as we look,
dancing, or simply standing
close enough to be touched by another's eyes,
too much static,
too many fears and expectations.
No one knows our flaws like we do,
no matter if we speak them.
And when it happens
that you catch sight of yourself,
the *you* always suspected,
but never seen,
that moment is a revelation,
mars and scars seem to blend away,
and all that counts
is a shine in the eyes,
a tilt to your chin,
or a lilt in the laughter
you always wanted to hear,
mindless and happy
then recognized for something amazing . . .
your own.

❧ TONY BENNETT AND YOU

"Hi honey . . .
Not much . . .
Thought we'd stay in tonight
since it's raining
and if you don't mind
a little Tony Bennett,
I don't mind
a spin or two around the floor,
just an excuse you understand,
to hold you close
and lay my head on your shoulder

The cat will think us crazy,
but really I don't care.
Oh, and if you're inclined
to take down my hair
and give me a place
to play hide and seek
with your kiss,
well . . . o.k.

No, I don't object
to you listening for my heart
when Tony is crooning for us
but I warn you sir,
you will absolutely *have* to stop that
in an hour or two."

❧ NOT QUITE NO

Please don't mention my neck.
Because when you do,
I can almost feel
warm lips caressing my nape,
parting softly to take
a taste,

and having sampled
that small spot,
I know you will want to bite
the soft skin of my shoulders
ever so lightly,
because you like it
when I whimper
and I know if I begged,
you would let my hair down,
step away,
and grin in my face
until I begged again . . .
for one more taste.

☙ Too Serious

I am too damned serious to smile,
So you can stop . . . really.
And don't give me that look,
you know . . . the one that says, "who me?"
because we both know you do it.
Two seconds after hello
the smile arrives
and doesn't leave
till long after your goodbye.
I am too serious to grin,
and you damned well know it,
so why do you insist
on catching me off guard?
How do you slip under the radar every time,
and why do I end up smiling
just because you looked me in the eye
and said, "Hello Beautiful?"
I really am too damned serious
for things like that.
Really, I am.

❧ Pay Attention

You only get so many chances Bucko,
so listen good.
That little girl is crying
because she says you don't listen,
or understand,
and she wants to know where her daddy is,
the one who swung her in his arms
when she was five,
and it seemed no one was near as wonderful.
Well, *Daddy*, this isn't about us.
This is about the best thing in your life,
and now is not the time
to be Mr. Hard-ass.
Catch her
before she runs,
before you cease to matter in her world,
before she doesn't need you to listen . . .
or I will not be the only one
you lose to your pride.

❧ Other Colors

Silvered moon falls to gray eyes,
this is what they mean by moonbeams,
light that feels like a touch
falling like prismatic mist on the skin.
Am I wanted as a woman,
or simply a woman wanted?
Do you know the difference
between the two?

Paled in moonlight,
you never met my like
but the song in my blood
is one you knew

long ago when firelight
cast harsh shadows
and transformed faces
into stone masks.

You always walk the pine path,
your step easy on the earth
keeping to solitary fire.

So why have you come, seeker
to the circles where I dance
as I ever have . . . alone?

❧ Far Afield Of Dreams

You made me blush
with the suggestion of uncovered toes,
though the grass was more lush
than any carpet
and in that instant
the thought of feeling it
against naked soles
was far more than tempting.

I took off those sandals
and dared not meet your eye
for the flush of pure pleasure
shot through me like a rainbow.
Yes, this was an old sensation
made new by your presence.
Whatever would you think
of a woman my years
crowing with delight
at her suddenly joyful feet?

But you weren't done . . . no.
You pointed out the low-lying mist
and the fireflies dancing inside it
like a Tolkien dream,
bade me inhale the scent

of countless small flowers
drugging the senses,
and asked me to trust you
while I breathed it all in.

Then you put a taste on my tongue
that shot me back in time
to the boardwalk, the midway,
the surf crashing on the sand
and a kiss stolen
by the one
you would have gladly given for free,
while one shooting star
blazed across your eyelids
to mark the moment
forever in a life's heart.

☙ Mulled Music

Nat King Cole is singing about my name,
and just that quick
I can feel your arms
slipping around me;
not possessive,
just a gentle reminder
that I am here,
you happened near
and your touch is not fire,
just sweet inspiration.

Your look is the kiss
you wanted to press to me
when I happened there
and you could smell White Shoulders
for just an instant.
Mulled music sweet with horns,
suddenly every note
smells like your cologne,

every word tastes like cognac . . .
and I am mulling
more than the sounds
while Nat sings me again
to that place in your arms
you made mine.

ଓଃ STEALTH

I was fitted with a personal Aegis system.
Nothing was going to fly under my radar,
not a butterfly or a bird,
and my seams were *tight*, damn-it.

But you sir, are brand new technology
never included in the schematics.
The designer of this system
did not have you in mind.

So just when I thought
I was safe and happy
you zoomed in,
multiple bogies,
and evaded everything I set up,
until I was left
breathless
terrified,
and wondering
how I ever expected
a stealth system
to protect me from being
laid bare
leaving me naked
and plain in your sight.

☙ Truth To God

I am enrapt, entangled
caught up in your words, your heart
and held close to a soul
I feel I have always known.

You fear what you say
will not serve me,
that there will always be more
I might need.

But words have a power that completes the soul
nurtures the strip-mined heart
and feeds the aching spirit.
All this you have done, and more.

Truth to God,
it is you I needed,
to wrap me in something new and warm
so that passion would become more than a pretty word.
Desire grew a knife-edge, sweet and sharp
and left its mark on me like no lover
I have ever known.

Your name is the one my heart whispers
when the night is deepest
and sleep still outraces me.
You are the one I reach for in quiet joy,
or mad frustration.
You I ask the gods to bless
when the silent voice of my soul
speaks to the all in prayer.

Truth to God, I will love you
with profound, simple conviction
and every dawn will bring you to me
in that first moment when the morning birds
find their calls.

You are a fundament of my soul,
and I would banish the doubt,

the fear, the old feelings
that make you wonder if this is real . . .
if I am real . . . if we could really be.

❧ SACRED DANCE

The virgin cannot yield more than innocence,
cannot give what she does not yet know.
Touch that is mere sensation,
tactile teasing of the skin
knows nothing of the subtle steps
taught to the learned by the gods.

In a life, there is but one giving,
one taker for such gifting,
and before you learn the steps
of the sacred dance
you must get to the place beyond flesh,
where eye to eye with the chosen
you can peel back the layers
you draped like veils
and slip into a naked beyond bare skin,
facing the fear of flame
facing the fear of yourself.

It was mine to give this,
some hidden part deep beneath
cleft, or breasts, or lips.
Hiding the secret of the taking
that I was born knowing,
but learned to fear.
One Giving.
One Taking.
And the act will seal you
for all time to the soul
who teaches you the sacred dance,
sings to your blood the cadence

the one who is the other half
of all you have been, or known.

Recognition full electric
pulsing without touch,
souls that seep through lost lives,
and force the mouth to the words
I *know* you.
Take me to the *yes* beyond consent,
where the open of thighs
is just the start,
all virgin ground inside of me,
music un-played,
movement unplanned,
unwind the skein of who I am,
and take me
to who I will be.

I ask of you the sacred dance,
profane to any eyes but ours,
too holy to be committed
to any but these two spirits,
and I will not fear what you will do,
when it was the gods
who asked this,
who lay me in your arms,
who long since named this day
that I would be taken
yielding absolutely,
and only to you.

☙ 10,000 Miles

That song will bring me tears
wrapped in a scarlet ribbon,
scented with you,
lavender and bittersweet regret.
Hard to not yearn for

the memories of us,
talking
laughing for hours,
and falling easily into each other
when love was an undercurrent
to every blessed word.

I should not weep
for the might-have-been's,
should not rage
that this moment,
closer than you have been in a lifetime,
there is yet distance between us.
But my heart was meant to hold you,
and my arms are heavy
from waiting so long outstretched
for one who never took
the last step to fill them.

Is it enough for you
that I am a pretty spirit,
a blithe ghost who whispers to your dreams?
After all that we have been,
you wonder at this stubborn pride of mine,
this petty caprice . . .
say that I know you love me.
All true.
But I am queen of nothing
so long as you are a life away,
and ten miles
or ten thousand makes little difference
when I long for one touch
from the soul that claimed me.

ଘ A Girl Like You

It had been a quiet, sweet night,
a shared bottle of wine,
and a man with a hollow heart
explaining why he cried
when he took his kids home
after a weekend with daddy.
I listened
murmured in all the right places,
and when it seemed a good idea,
offered a massage to ease him.
He was not my lover,
didn't think of me like that,
and the touching was innocent
at least for him.
He could never see my face
as I worked on the knots and tangles
sadness had made of his shoulders and neck.
We talked intimately,
and I felt him go easy under my hands.
Suddenly he looked up at me,
a broad smile on his face,
and asked if I knew how wonderful I was,
gentle
kind
unique
a real treasure . . .
and then he said,
I swear to god he uttered these words,
"Why can't I meet a girl like you?"
My face froze.
Ice lodged in my heart and throat.
A girl like me?

Twenty-five years later
and my face burns with it still.
Why in the world did he need

a girl like me,
when the original was there for the taking?

But the story didn't quite end there.
Months later
when our sweet nights became few,
I looked
elsewhere for what he could not offer.
I fell in love with another man
who liked me just fine the way I was.
The fool came back
and decided that I was a girl like me after all.
He caught me with a kiss
that said I wasn't his sister
pressed against me hard
and looked at me with raw need
for the very first time.
I looked back and told him
that I couldn't possibly
because he never could manage to love
a girl like me.

ଓଃ Not So Easily Broken

Girl,
I know you are hurting deep,
and your spectrum is rich
in black, red and indigo
but you've been there and back,
forty days in the desert,
and here you are.
It's not that you are perfect
but you are strong
yes,
strong is a bitch
but it beats the hell
out of hoping for rescue
when you're sinking for the third time.

Caught in a riptide
your only option:
to swim away from the shore,
and pray like hell
that when you're clear
you can swim back.
But girl,
you are not so easily broken.
Flawless
unscarred
without mark or wound
just means untried.
In our tribe,
the only marks that count
are battle scars,
not the cuts we give ourselves
to see if we can still feel.
Scoop up the love
that falls around you like rain
and drink it deep.
We are not so easily broken,
you or I.
Now come sister,
paint my face for the next battle
and if you wish,
I will paint yours.

❦ SPEAKING TO THE SLEEPING HEART

Ah love, you are caught in the bedclothes
of emotion.
The linens of your life
have twisted around your ankles
making you believe you are caught.
In your sleep,
you chafe, turn, fret
and are loathe to speak

of my habits with blankets
for fear of wounding my waking self.
So I will gently tug, and smooth,
set things to right
cover you lightly,
and snug the pillows around you
so you feel safe, but free . . .
then curl up beside you
and wait for the morning
knowing that maybe not today,
and maybe not tomorrow,
but sleep will give you up to me,
when you are ready to open your eyes
to the lover
who whispered softly to your sleeping heart
when it was tired,
and in need of peace.
Dream sweet . . .

ଔ When The Heart Decides

Funny
we expect the big moments of our lives
to arrive like the burning bush
in a Cecil B. De Mille extravaganza,
so there is no mistaking
when a change has been made
that will alter us forever.
But that is a lie.
It's the small changes,
minute things that change our worlds,
and our hearts
beyond recognition.
The very first "I love you"
spoken with quiet conviction,
a baby's first coo,
the last breath

of a heart you dearly love.
Such little things,
but immense in their way,
life changing,
soul sorting,
significant, if only to us.
There comes that moment
when the heart decides, and
quietly sets you on your path
without fanfare, or trumpets.
So subtle
that half the time
you cannot even recall the instant.
Funny.
We will remember the conflict,
the weighing,
the whole process of decision,
but almost never recognize
the moment when the heart decided.
Luckily, I was paying attention
the moment my heart spoke your name
so softly,
but in a way that brooked no argument.
For once,
the cacophony of my days
did not drown out
the most important second
I have ever known.
When my heart decided.

☙ Plaster, Putty And Spackle

"You have not spoken to me in two months."

I was startled, hearing those words,
not because of the anger
that was surely there,
but the hurt.

Surely he was mistaken,
but as I thought back,
I knew the truth:
that I had become silent.

I had my reasons,
but for once
I buried the anger,
anger I have till now
made no attempt to conceal.
I looked at him,
felt the hurting,
and it stunned me.

Long ago, I assumed
you did not care.
Often enough
you railed at my chatter,
and yes, even asked
if I had to talk so much.
I could have taken the cheap route,
and flung angry words at you,
watch you cringe,
and win some petty victory.
But that would have lost the war.

So I followed you to bed
where you lay cold and stiff,
and I put my arms around you,
reaching across a chasm
that had grown,
inches, feet, yards wide.
I let you talk
and did not turn it back on you,
even when you tried to erase
the part you made in the battle.
No recriminations,
no hissing,
no flinging of verbal vitriol
in self-defense.

We once had a foundation
I would have sworn
was made of granite.
Only now,
the house is shabby,
and leaning,
the walls are cracked,
and it looks like nothing I remember.

I have plaster,
putty
and spackle.
I want to fix
at least what I can.
Too much has fallen
while I waited
for you to start repairs.

I swear by the love
that together we grew,
never once
did I mean to hurt you.
If the house falls,
at least I will have tried.
I never knew
you needed me to speak,
did not feel like I mattered.
I pulled my heart away
and did not think you would care.

Your turn to talk,
I will listen.
And while I do,
I will glue the leg of this chair,
try to banish the cobwebs,
and move closer to where you are.
Maybe then we will know
if plaster, putty, and spackle
can save the foundation
we began with love.

☙ Sharing Water

When a man dries a woman's tears
and gentles her with a touch
born of love,
I call that *sharing water*.

When his fingers brush her hair,
and his mouth finds hers
to quiet a tremble of despair,
I call that *sharing water*.

When his lips sip her tears,
and he pulls her near
to warm the numb of her heart
I call that *sharing water*.

When a man gives softly,
finds a tiny flame
and his heart fans it
with beat matched to beat,
I call that *sharing water*.

When it costs him heart and soul
to remind her of living,
when life is a distant seeming dream,
there is nothing to do
but lace together fingers,
reach out with a spirit,
and share water
with the sweet dreamer
who taught the heart to love.

❦ Cedar Wood And Cinnabar

Cedar wood and cinnabar,
memory has a scent,
love has a feel,
and tender is the word
for a touch to self or soul.
The spirit once touched
will never be the same.
It takes the print,
altering slightly
to couch a heart
offered in innocent truth.
I breathe in rare woods,
and feel you
curled softly against my being,
Solomon's cedars
scenting the air,
reminding me of his song
and the love he held immortal.
What is, is.
What will be, simply a wisp of dream.
It is enough that I love,
and find love in return.
But still I would be
the smell of cedar wood and cinnabar
to your heart.

❦ Soft Words On A Rainy Night

Words spoken like sweet balm,
could almost taste the tang of the mint,
feel the sticky of honey,
soft-voiced soothing,
save for the ones you caressed.

I hide the catch of my breath
when you held one word or other
in the flat of your hand.
Not teasing, this . . .
more a subtle tasting of the mind,
and no, you never touched me . . . quite.

But I went to my sheets
aware of the skin
I so often take for granted,
scolded my foolish fancy,
but still shut my eyes
smiling.

ଔ READING EROTICA ALONE

You read those words
and feel a pang,
knowing all too well the meaning.
Where do you take the belly burn
the dreadful soft ache
when you read the words alone?

When there is a touch you desire,
a yearning to turn fiction into delicious
a spirit to give soul to flesh,
to make a joining
instead of a rutting,
where do you turn
when you read the words alone?

Lonely is a dance for the heart,
but the flesh craves someone whole
who can give voice and spark
to more than heat,
someone to stand before
naked to the soul,
with shining eyes,

lips softly parted,
and utterly without fear.

But where is this lover,
this dream
this angel
when you are there,
reading erotica alone?

ଔ Knowing

Once a woman has touched your flesh,
caught your attention
in a way frankly erotic,
you can never look at her again,
never hear her voice,
and not remember
her taste.

You can try for *friendly* lover status,
it might be easy, breezy-light,
but let another man touch her,
and watch for the green-eyed monster
at the thought
she might be taken by other flesh.

Past touch does not vanish,
she can never forget
how it felt
when you filled her at first,
she can never look in your eyes,
and fail to think of the unasked kiss
she found herself tasting.

So never take to your bed
a friend you don't mean to keep as a lover,
because the knowing
the touch,
the taste
will never go away,

and there is no going back to friends
once she has tasted your seed,
once you have sunk into her body,
no matter how noble the intention.

The knowing remains.

⌘ Pleasure Gardens Of The Gods

They choose from the fairest,
the most skilled,
those who would be consort to the Pharaoh,
but untouched even by the Living God,
made man by Ra,
and kissed by the lips of Isis.
Once sealed to Ra,
this one would never be defiled
by the eyes of man,
never desecrated by their touch.

The Sealing was one day,
and one night
spent in the arms of the God,
so if her belly swelled with his seed,
she would be sacred among women,
pampered,
fed only the choicest morsels
and her merest whim made law.
The flesh of the god
between her thighs
would elevate her above all.

But that one day
would be paid for
with a life of isolation,
more carefully guarded
than any temple priestess.
She would never again be touched
unless the God came to her in dreams.

Oh sweet the touch of the godhead,
many the pleasures of the night,
open to the touch,
alive,
breasts hard and sweet to aching,
succulent,
the juice of the pomegranate
red on the lips of Ra,
she will float,
soar,
be taken again and again
till she is sealed
to his skin for all time.

The dawn will come,
and the serving girls
will feed her supine,
so that no seed is spilled.
For one more day
she will be strong
with the scent of the god,
fed,
fanned,
sung to,
bathed
in milk and honey,
rinsed with sweet wine,
then wrapped in linen
sandaled in gold-chased kid,
and led to her new home
where she will spend her life
pining for the touch
of the divine.

✿ Tasting Breath

You always look in my eyes
before our lips touch, and
defy me to close mine
against the rush of sensation
that sweeps me.
You want to see the pleasure,
the shock,
want to sink into the gray-green
so I will know
who is touching me,
tasting me,
sipping my breath like heady wine
served to compliment the perfect meal,
or cleanse the palate between courses.

Sweet,
moist,
drugged,
I flow into your arms
without hesitation,
drape myself around you,
lean against you with a soft sigh
and wonder how it is
that your kiss
carries me home
every time,
makes me into someone beautiful,
raises me to passion,
then tucks me sweetly to sleep
warding me from pain or harm.
This lip on lip,
tender touching
is balm,
sweet elixir
the stuff of alchemy
and the gift that only you can give.

❧ The Touch

I had never seen the match flare in your eyes,
never felt the white-blue lick of simple awareness
or felt the tactile brush of spirit fingers
seeking to loose my hair.
Never saw the look turn to hunger
so sharp I could taste your mouth
like new wine
from lips to lids,
tracing my chin,
giving me the touch that comes
before a touch knows it is coming.

How to answer those eyes,
when a glance down or away
might be interpreted as "no,"
the hesitation is only surprise
a moment to adjust to the glow,
light you began with a spark
that shines two layers beneath my skin.

The sweet hot wax of a glance,
warming where it falls,
the shift in attention,
the laughter falling to silence
beneath the weight of a touch
that is only your eyes.
When did I go from a woman you knew,
to one you wished to know?

If I ever questioned how you saw me,
I do not question now.
Your hand may suddenly rise,
your fingers finally seek
to know if I am really as delicious
as your eyes have imagined.
How to answer the frank look,
as if my own eyes knew the steps to this tango
when my insides are every bit the wallflower

of fifteen,
the first time a man looked at me;
eyes I wanted to meet and melt
as if I knew the wiles I only wished.

But those eyes are yours.
Now I feel them seeking
for the hard thud beneath the cloth,
as if you could feel the instant
something in me murmured your name.
Not a gentle teasing smile,
not a simple *bon ami*
but just your eyes
seeing me as a woman
you need to love
who bade you close the distance
between visual and tactile certainty,
with one look I never saw coming.

☙ EVENTIDE

Not so much maudlin in moonlight,
or softly swirled in sleep-sand,
but the mosaic-eyed dreamer,
summoned to subconscious
by the madrigal voice
that hums to a life.

The soft sound of a pen scratching,
words cut into soul parchment,
and I know how he cuts his own quills,
needle sharp,
so the tattoo will never fade.

I heard him stir at eventide,
face wreathed by smoke,
eyes fixed on something aglow
just beyond true vision
soul possessed by sinner and angel,

trading sword for the mightier pen,
moonlight dervish
whirling within the hope of love,
the tinge of lust,
dreams eleven lifetimes birthing.

He must craft at eventide
when the stars bestow their silence,
when the world is asleep,
and the soul can walk alone,
all the while reaching,
searching
sifting
for the one who made ripe the words
of eventide.

☙ OLD SEER IN TARTARUS

When you are simply not believed,
or when the telling of a truth
will cost you a piece of your heart,
you learn to be silent
and sin by omission,
hiding in plain sight
and pretend that it's just fine,
the bits of you that go unnoticed,
and untouched.

It's worth the sip of those waters,
to forget burning need,
to forget yet another heart
set aside.
Yes, I am precious as friend,
but that is the limit of the need.
I know I will be eclipsed,
shadowed
forgotten
that is the way of it.

Immortal never for love,
and best remembered
for being thought mad or a liar.
Dip the cup quickly,
that I might drink a toast
to all the tiny wants and needs,
that were never mine to fill.
Let me be just another silent shade
in the cool still of Tartarus.

☙ QUESTIONING THE CELESTIAL

I dab perfume on 14 points
not to thrill your senses,
but to awaken my own.
I deal the cards for a 9-card draw,
they speak their own language.
You have questions
they taste like doubt
and I hear, "What if ?"
like a cackled incantation
that makes the small hairs dance
on the back of my neck.
Am I goddess to you, or witch?
I whisper to myself the trick
of holding close, without holding too tight,
warn myself against too many *I love you's*
and wonder what it is I can possibly do
to make you feel me as real,
if after white light, amber glaze,
love, life, laughter, lust and tears
you could possibly wonder
if I will just walk away from you
without a backward glance.
You say that perhaps you are too much . . .
but is not the other half of that question
that perhaps I will not be enough?

I will brew tea with loose leaves,
look for your face
in the bottom of the cup,
and perhaps find your answers there.
But for now I will pull the shawl
more tightly around my shoulders
and pretend that I am much wiser a gypsy
than my heart knows me to be.

❧ PLAINER WORDS

I have received fancier invites,
calligraphy on vellum,
wax sealed to perfection,
that offered merely a night,
perhaps two, of stultifying diversion.
But this was less than a dozen words,
ending in a question,
as casual as could be.

So knowing me now as well as you do,
how far afield I will range to avoid foolish,
how deeply I fear dumb,
or how succinct my desire to avoid stupid;
I know that no matter how I tried
for casual,
I came off like a gushing girl child.

And all the while as I tiptoed through
the human minefield of your being,
I did not say what I was thinking:
that you seemed somehow familiar,
better known than I could credit.
I depended on the plainer words,
not the poetry, for my cues.

Near to a year gone by,
and I could never explain
how you became who you are,

or how I became
a safe place for you to rest
between bouts.
I only know that it all began
with plainer words than some might credit,
and something that glimmered
in pale recognition
against the silence of a soul's night.

I cannot say you *became* dear,
because somehow, you always were.
With you the challenge
is not to say the pretty things,
but the plainer words
you've come to expect
from a voice you
knew long before
you knew the voice
I now call my own.

◊ Transubstantiation

You take the leavings of a soul,
vapor trails from a touch that was,
whispers of words so long faded
that there is not even an echo
save the captured essences you view;
you take these gossamer ghosts,
pull them through the sieve of your soul,
trace them to a timeline of real,
and make them dance
in something like flesh,
until they can be seen,
felt
touched
and I do not know
if you were called
to tempt the spirits,

or are simply the one
who speaks the tongue
of so many lives
that you cannot help but hear them
when the *I love you* spoken
belongs to an ancient night
you once called your own.

ൣ SIROCCO

Safe here the words,
force of nature,
fallen angel
here you do not tread,
so here I can speak it.

Whirlwind pulsing through
of all the words spoken,
how often do you hear "no?"

Once it may have maddened me
that you saw me as a mirror,
but now there is safety there.

Better to be the smoked glass
that casts your reflection,
than an element I cannot touch
without loss of limb,
or sanity.

I wish to word the one question
haunting me dreaming or awake.

What am I to you,
why do I feel you like a second self,
why does it seem
I am just the next ghost
you have chained with love,
afraid I might stay,
but more afraid I might go?

ℂℜ Birth Of Self

Called to witness the birth,
pangs suffered in grim silence
not what you once were,
not yet who you will be,
and I am midwife to a soul,
can only mop gently at the beaded brow,
speak calm words
and watch the tremors
rack your form,
wondering what healing
will take you beyond the gaping gates
of a uniquely personal hell.

Pain that does not ease,
an inchoate rage
that the words do not cleanse,
that the ulcer still roils,
and the gray light of dawn
is ever the dimmest hope
to those who torment
in the long lean hours of night.

You do not fear the shades, but you
poured the blood offering to summon them,
and then anguish that the only words
permitted betwixt living and dead
are the ones already spoken,
flesh-to-flesh.
I am but the midwife.
I can urge
calm,
but quiet and comfort
will not be yours
until you finish the labor
you began all unknowing.

❧ Certain Knowledge

When the seeker invokes the softly spoken,
when the light of day is simply gray passage
to the coming of a wine-dark night,
when the stars slow to the eye,
and the all is in perfect silence
comes the time of Certain Knowledge,
when the old gods speak best.

Hints and glints of a tongue long faded,
a sound that recalls a touch
and faces we do not forget
no matter that life has lost them.
We seek the knowing of absolute,
cradle the past in our arms
like an infant never born,
but longed for,
dreamt about,
and named to our hearts.

We reach for certain knowledge,
with hands that tremble,
seeking to bury the doubt
before the last sheet is drawn,
to know what it is,
why we are,
and how ghosts became a comfort,
in tempestuous times,
how we spent our minutes
as if we would not one day count them,
hoard them,
kiss each one
like a child we were doomed to lose.

Comes the time of certain knowledge,
when all we gave to regret
is measured, and weighed,
then given its due dignity
passed through pomp and ceremony,

settled to a price, never what we reckoned, or guessed,
and always more than we wished to pay.

Comes the time when the mist lifts
and wishes or dreams fade to words
we breathed to dawn, or dusk,
when we are looking at the correct place
and sky is just a map of the cosmos
imprinted with our lives.

Then you hear the voice
that says you will never know all, but perhaps in time,
you will know enough
to make a true reckoning
of the skin we were given to dance in,
for the ticks we counted as lives,
for all the questions the old gods
ignored because they had already answered.

☙ Candle To A Life

He said we are but candles
waiting to be gutted,
or stilled,
and while he is a wise one,
who saw many more wars
than even I can guess,
my still voice says different.

Those we held, and those we knew
pass from our lives
so much against our will,
we would hold them here and fast forever,
lavish in their touch
and never let them get on
with their place in the cosmos.

How we long for goodbye,
regret the said, and unsaid,
curse and bless the places they stood,

and always reach for them
in times of need.

At times the grief or longing
for the much loved
we keen to ourselves,
and rock inside
dulling our hearts to the touch that still can be,
the touch that still is.

I say no candle will ever be cold
that held the flame of love,
and I say that no one
is something so brief as a candle flame.
So, wise old warrior with heart-heavy eyes,
do not let the scars
make you miss the lightest touch,
that reminds us of what, and who, and when
there was a candle to hold to our lives.

☙ Healing Craft

When you see a ragged tear
in the spirit or the heart,
you begin to wonder how much silk
or catgut it will take
to tie off the worst.

You try to keep the stitches
small and neat,
so you don't think
about how much your needle
must be hurting.

You remind yourself that a nasty wound
will rarely heal without help.

You pack the rend
with herbs to cleanse
try not to feel the wince,

try to speak of other things
while you close a wound
and pray that it will hold.

Maybe there will be a scar, yes
but function is more important
than pretty,
when it's healer craft you do.

So much depends on the heart,
the grit,
the will to live . . .
something you tell yourself each day,
as if that will save you
when one slips through
and makes you feel
like you failed
the very light that guides you.

ೞ TREMBLE

An intellectual discussion
on a small word . . .
such a loaded word
from where I sit.

So many things that *tremble* can mean,
or suggest;
not fear exactly, something
more delicate than that.

When I am afraid, I shake,
bone deep and wracking.

When I am angry,
it comes in waves
and I vibrate.

But few things make me *tremble*,
and all of them are dangerous.

Tremble means my heart is involved,
tremble means I have been touched,
tremble means I should not go there,
and always
tremble means I already have.

❧ Dancing Lessons

The girl that was not me
(not my face),
led hobbling, while black shirts sneered
at her limping progress.
I could see the braces
on her legs
(my legs),
feel the cut of the metal,
almost smell the brown leather straps
that tried to right
what polio had done to her
(to me),
felt the shame,
wolf eyes were on her,
laughing at the wound
she tried never to see.
Cripple is a cruel word,
but she had gotten used
(I had)
to hearing it whispered.
But only rarely jeered
never with such hatred.
She tried not to cry
(I tried)
as they led her to the spot,
metal post driven into the ground
waist high,
tried not to wince
(because they might do worse)

as leather cut her wrists
and she heard them say
(I heard)
"time for the dancing lesson girl,"
and a moment later
the bucket came.
A splash
She smelled the kerosene
(I smelled it),
did not understand
how evil it would be
(I felt it).
A moment later a match was struck
and the girl flared
image burned in my soul
as she tried to pull away
and fell to her knees
(my knees)
and there was no more
but the screaming when I woke
at all of six years old
and knew that once, I had died
because I was not
a madman's dream of perfect.

ॐ WHITE MARBLE ANGELS

One afternoon spent
searching for white marble angels
one man's art
spent to honor a life now ended.
When you see them,
you stop to
ponder the skill that shaped the marble
and wonder why this life
or that love
demanded more than the flat marker

making do for most.
Angels, arms outstretched in welcome,
or was it the need
for one last touch,
one last word
one last whispered
Oh, please no . . . not yet
wept by a heart
that marked that spot
with something that said,
"Oh god,
how I loved you . . ."

☙ Waiting Is

The deep silence of the uncalled line,
the sigh that rings to the bones,
the feeling of wanting to leap
while the feet are still caught in kudzu chains.

Waiting is
the last patch of bramble stickers
betwixt you and the heart
no way around,
just through
with gritted teeth
knowing the blood will flow,
knowing the nerves will shriek
but knowing you must.

Waiting is
the bell that sounds in the blood
when I hear
or speak
or think your name
with the reverence
of a pilgrim

just steps away
from the Saints' gate.

Waiting is
what love has become
waiting
for you to be.

⌘ BATTERED OLD BLUES

He always carries the old leather case,
nicked, dented and worn.
When he opens it
to show off the old stringed wonder,
the velvet is frayed to ghostly in spots,
fading to pale from once crimson glory.

The tuning knobs are yellowed ivory,
from nights of soft coercion
to just the proper tone
and though he never said it,
you know this guitar has a name . . .
a woman's name.

His fingers slide and glide.
You watch his hands in silence
as he picks a tune at random
from the play list in his heart;
maybe a song that never had words
till he thought to add them.
And that never-heard song
strikes a chord of pained wonder.

You can almost see her,
the old Gibson's namesake,
gifting the shadows with a near smile,
then fading into shade
just as his voice hitches
on the piece of his heart
that she carries in a locket

from back in the days
that she awaited
his battered old blues.

❧ Recognition

You did not speak the name,
that I only saw wreathed in smoke,
as I stepped with both feet
on the grave I knew
too many lifetimes ago.

I did not look in your eyes
as I felt her stir, and turn, and sigh,
giving her to my skin
so she could breathe again,
and knew for once and all
that I could not keep dodging
every time I felt the phantom
that says I knew you.

At least I am not alone.
I have her for company,
and now you.
She keeps your secrets,
and follows you with calm eyes,
but there is grieving to her,
the tang of sad regret,
unspoken anguish
of the one she cannot name,
but does not forget
even these lifetimes past.

They say two people
cannot be the same kind of crazy,
but I am left with recognition,
and wonder when I will have the courage
to let her speak your name.

☙ Fractured Self

Do not ask me where I have been,
for words cannot touch
the feeling of being torn apart
from the outside in,
a journey purchased
by a sin ages old before my birth.

A voice not mine, but so familiar,
a name I never knew
suddenly feels all too true
and I am spinning back,
spiraling to touch the fabric
of a place my bones know.

This is the first life.
How could they call me wise
when I was just begun,
the bruja of a tribe?
How could she claim innocence
when the guilt bent her near double
in my mind's eye?

The smoke hangs below
the crest of the night
winter cold, spangled with stars
so cold,
the moon's face a screaming woman
with features I know
all too well.

I see it all,
from the eye of the crow
and that quickly becomes myself,
all these lives later.
Dream,
illusion,
vision?
I cannot say.

But my fingers find a streak of pure white
that yesterday had never seen.
No, I beg you,
do not ask where I have been.

ଏଷ Tussie-Mussie

Lavish layered in lavender,
love left in lace of grand eloquence
and every shared touch shimmers
with the soft words as batting.

Flowers dried to perfect stasis,
still whiff with want and wonder
and the perfume is redolent
with the musk of time.

You will open the box but rarely,
peel back the wrappings
with the tender of a lover,
and for a moment that scent
will carry you to absent arms,
in one taunt tease of time.

A tussie-mussie made of wishes,
a bouquet of secret dreams . . .
you will speak her name
only to the latest hour,
when the moon silvers all,
even the heart you placed
within the layers of lavender,
for memory.

❧ Moon Dancing

The lake was mirror flat,
lacking only the silver.

Not a wrinkle or a ripple
just my face reflected in cedar water,
waiting for the sky maiden
to begin her dance.

Feeling a different sort of old,
I dropped the years
one by one in the water,
not surprised when the surface
swallowed them whole.

All the weight
that slipped from me
raised the level not at all.

Silly mortal . . .
did you think your days
meant a thing to a place
that has always been?

That thought was meant as sad,
but then I laughed
not from absurdity,
but the fact that I was waiting
to talk to the moon,
when there were plenty of stars
just waiting to dance for me.

And when she came
resplendent as always
filling eyes and heart with wind chime waltzes,
it became a circle dance of the season.

I was not tired;
I was not old,
just ready for the fireside
and the softly whispered dreams

of the flame elemental
who knew that I would come
when I had danced at last my fill.

❧ Echoes Of Rain

The rain by the lake is different,
not a business-like downpour,
but more a lacks-a-day-sickle splatter
that calms and soothes,
says you are warm,
and dry.

The wood-smoke tang
tickles my nose,
the smell of coffee fresh brewed
ready to bite my tongue,
and the mist on the water
whispers like a naughty child in my ear
that I could be out there
catching raindrops on my face.
What does it matter
that I am supposed to be
all grown up?

I hear the sounds,
breathe the scent of wet woods
rowdy with rhododendron,
and the cedar and pine
kiss me like a new lover,
in this quiet place.

But my eyelids
need to feel the wet,
my skin is thirsty for mist,
my eyes are starved
for the moon that will rise
and flirt with the earth
through gossamer clouds.

And all I will feel
standing there in the elements,
is the sweet blessing of the day
when the sound I love best
layered with the crackle of the fire
is the echo of the rain
that knows every name
I have ever been.

⊂⊃ Exigency

Seclusion not sought,
and yet thicker the walls
shutting out sound and light
feeling the bricking,
mortar dried hard now,
so all I hear are echoes
and the thin rasp of my own breathing.

Once I might have been freed of this,
once I could have stepped away,
but my heart could not bear
that another pay for my choosing.
So I willed myself to calm
even as another stone
slid softly into place.

This cairn grew around me,
like moss on a shade tree,
like the lichen on too still a rock,
the tears will not melt the stones,
cries will not break the brick,
and I will be shut unto myself.

I gave myself to this half-life.
Now I cannot bear
to feel the beating of my heart
so loud in my ears,
not quite dead,

just alive enough
to rail against premature burial,
to hate the flowers left in tribute,
and to know I still love the light
too well to settle for darkness.

⌘ THE TIME OF CHILDREN

To each life will come the ticking moment
when childhood slides into Styx.
For each there is a catalyst
never guessed or expected.

We are never prepared
for the thing that stamps *paid*
on the halcyon hours,
shutting firmly the door
of what we were in innocence.

Violet twilight bringing tidings
of something the heart had guessed,
but logic denied until the choked words
spoke a grim truth too plainly.

Suddenly the flirting time
half man, half child
ends in cold, tearing grief;
searing a soul and sealing in it
a torment too long unspoken.

Not many can count the hour,
mark the moment,
know with bone-deep certainty
the instant their childhood died . . .
but I know one other who did.

Just now,
the mute witness gives tongue
to the weeping rage,
the harsh abandonment,

the loss dull and keen
that flash-forged a soul,
and carried a life through its days,
but never again knew
the glistening dew
of the perfect rose
cut minutes before its moment
of full living glory.

ℭℜ Shaman

I was called without intention,
swept into this skin
a moment before dying,
and that is how they say
the shaman is born in each.

The smell of life is rich and high,
electric in my nostrils,
drugging the sense of now
till it falls away like the first petals.

The pulse becomes a drum measure
flooding the blood till time shatters
and all that has been
becomes one with all I have known.

Healer is but part,
now I am called to the mysteries,
skin over skin,
there is in me
something dancing to the Cosmos,
calling to the night air,
seeking to read the flare of night sky.

The taste of life and living so deep,
that I am awash with the tang,
feel the glow to my deepest cell,
the surety that at last
I have learned the name

that the stars only whispered
till I knew it for my own.

◑ THE SCRYING BOWL

You see only the light dappled,
catching hints there and here
that another might dance
within this mortal skin.
I call myself a gypsy
with a wry smile,
and confess a fear of dark places
you cannot comprehend,
but then you are not chained
in the same way, brother of night.

All my life I knew the ripples
when time folded to itself,
a face would seem deathly white
all others saw as pale,
and when the call came
it was never a shock to me,
deep shadows of the scrying bowl
where once I stood,
slave to eyeless sight.

At times I am uneasy,
for I feel another self lurking
just below the thinnest of my skin,
I do not look too close,
not because I fear,
but because I know she waits
to resume the task of ancient days.

I know the rose attar of her unguents,
and if I dance away
it is because she knows someone too well,
cares nothing for grace or pity,
and she longs to spin my skin

into the cloak she wore
beneath the merciless night,
when they called her priestess,
and all was there for her to see,
in the mirror of the scrying bowl
she hid in her soul.

☙ Touch Of An Old Soul

Your words cover my skin,
trapping a small beating creature
beneath my breasts,
between my ribs,
and dear God this owes nothing to lust,
less to thighs gone to jelly.

I cannot even imagine
the surrender you would demand.
I fear the hand touch of your soul,
that would slide unbidden
into this skin like so much smoke,
and force the creature out of me
that once danced beneath you
in another skin.

I have no idea, not an inkling
what of you she fears.
I only know that when you speak,
she twists inside my belly
half leaning toward you in delight,
half pulling away in fear.

If you were deep in me,
there would be nowhere
for my sweet revenant to hide,
because there is no bit of my body,
no taste,
no place that you will not plumb,
searching for the old soul

who lies asleep within me;
the old soul you wake
an inch at a time,
determined that *this* time,
you will not walk alone to Valhalla;
that *this* time,
I will give all I promised
when last I danced my hips
against the surging truth
of every man
you have ever been.

❧ STONE FLOWERS

Dappled dawn should be a broom,
sweeping away cobwebs,
banishing the beasties to unblessed graves,
and warming me for another day's life.
I feel the place,
small and gray and unformed
where sunlight and star-shine
never touch,
where I am the doppelganger,
and my life is smoke.
Here I am Egyptian
preparing for the journey,
hiding the writings as clues,
so my next self will know
how to steer the boat
that carries the newly born
to fresh life.

Believing the spirit does not die,
yet not trusting it
to remember the lessons of a life,
I will carry the stone flowers
to remind me
of what was real,

what was sweet,
and all I could not bear
to have to learn again,
when the Ka is journeying
to another place,
and leaving this form behind
like the last taste
of bittersweet love
on the tongue of the life I led.

❧ MEASURE AND MEANING

When a man gets to thinking
that the measure of a life
can be added up in minutes,
that the whole silly mess
is meaningless,
because we do not know
which breath will be our last,
he is calling in the chasm of himself,
and hating the echoes
that mock his meaning.

When a moment of quiet
is suddenly sixty seconds lost,
and a humble one asks again of God,
why am I,
the silence is not indifference.
It is not denial,
or rejection of the impertinent question.
The still is only the moment
that we are given
to listen more closely,
to the decimal places of ourselves.

We weigh all things,
even our hearts, to determine value.
And while you are listening

for the voice of your own,
while you are singing softly
to the tune no one else hears,
wondering if you can ever match
that delicate coda and countermeasure,
never forget that the song
you strain for
was always yours.

☙ Atlas And The Nine Ton Stone

You do not expect to find a titan
tucked in amongst humanity,
larger than life,
poised and balanced
solitary,
most times silent.
Rather we expect a titan
to speak with the voice of a god,
concealing any hint of human inflection.

I sensed him one night,
and turned to find him standing there,
a wry smile painted on his face
as he shifted to better support the weight.
He asked if I was surprised
that he resembled so much a mortal being.

I looked deep into those tired eyes,
and shook my head, slowly.
"Heroes are rarely the Rodin ideal,"
I answered.
"Any more than heroines
can be measured by the dazzle
of a toothpaste smile."

I saw how the weight he bore
twisted the corded muscles,
and it seemed impossible

that he would not falter,
surrender to the bulk
and allow it to crush him.

But when you carry a load,
putting it down
may give you a breather,
but then comes the moment,
you must take it up again . . .
and each time, it is harder
to bend the back,
to make the neck and shoulders
accept and form to the weight
of the nine ton stone.

We talked a while,
about simple things . . .
the laughter of children,
the importance of dreams,
and the fact that no one signs up
to bear the weight of the world.

No,
but somewhere, we tell ourselves
given the right inducement
we could bear the bulk
of a nine ton stone,
if never one as crushing as ten.

The gods, or God
laugh at us then . . .
because weight grows heavier with time.
Because you have to hold it always,
and *weary* does not matter,
and aching does not matter.

I did not flatter myself to think
I had eased the load
of this gentle titan with the too-mortal eyes,
that I had made him feel easy,
or even given him a short breather
to shift the weight for the next decade.

No, all I did
was discover a mortal glimmer,
and feel the solid beat
of an unflinching heart,
while giving him pause for just a moment
to think of something else,
something simpler
than the world he carries.

ଓଃ Mystic

Sanskrit written on the soul,
delicate words etched
with an artist's precision;
avant-garde flair.
Seeking the smaller words
for the larger truths,
turning with the wheel, within the wheel,
conversing with the universe
amused when others see the vastness,
but fail to hear the bells
that are the laughter.

Tears are the soft countermeasure,
marking where we stood in grief
making us believe that tears count
much more than the grin.
But, for one so wise
you labor too long,
toil too hard
and ignore your grant of peace.

☙ Wood Smoke And Witchery

I gather the small herbs,
dry the flowers on the hearth,
warm the incense
in a small clay jar . . .
all in readiness for the seeker
with questions of life
or God,
or perhaps just himself.

Eyes like an ocean,
heart like a wheel,
soul illuminated with other lives,
trembling before the stone.

What would you ask, mortal?
The old one sleeps inside me,
wearied, wary,
wise and withered,
she will ask nothing of you
that you do not already pay
with every indrawn breath.

Ask mortal . . .
and give freely to the question,
no half measures for the surety of your soul,
ask for the forgotten minutes
swirling again like wood smoke
in a dream of the last maddened angel,
sharp as the edge
of the sword drawn
against eleven kinds of loss.

Listen well mortal . . .
for you dare not leave this life
not knowing why it was chosen for you.
Ask . . . and stand ready
for the full weight of dreams
gone from wood smoke to flesh.

❧ All The Clever Words

What can a man say to the likes of me,
who made words my stock and trade,
cut my teeth on Shakespeare,
too wary of those who waxed poetic
when the topic was me?

I had armor against the clever words,
kept the mirror close
not because I was so lovely
but because I knew otherwise,
and when they praised more than my eyes,
I knew them for too smooth,
and knew they had said the same
to any woman with breasts and breath.

So what could a man say to catch this heart,
dressed in running shoes,
and standing at the mark,
all too ready to sprint away
if something falls too close?

Not clever words,
not poetry,
just things of singular truth,
plain in beauty
spoken with hesitation
as if he feared I would find him mad,
but matching word for word
the things I never said,
nor even whispered
in a thousand poems
written when I did not know
someone was listening
to the drum cadence of a heart,
or waiting for one perfect silence
to explain
what all the clever words
never knew to speak.

❧ STEPPING AWAY

We carried them everywhere at first;
in our arms,
in baskets,
holding them up
to learn about gravity,
trying to protect those chubby bottoms
from hitting too fast.

Then they crawled,
scooting along with purpose
and determination,
crowing with delight
when they could get there.

They hauled themselves up
on shaky legs,
holding onto us,
little lower lips thrust out.
They did not have the words,
but when they stood,
and took one step,
it was beyond JOY!

So tell me mother,
blinking back your tears,
that the very first time
your child took a step away,
that your heart did not lurch;
one small premonition,
we all quashed
because it was just too darned soon.
They were *babies*.

It was just one step.
Then another,
and they were toddlers,
who didn't seem to need us . . .
not every second.

But it felt good when they
came running back
to us,
to home.

They grew,
and each step they took
was further away.
When we looked
we saw our beautiful child
in *that* world,
knowing too well
what *that* world could do,
and we wanted to pull them back,
and say, "not yet Honey,
not so fast. Please?"

And it all led to now,
when the best gift a mother can give,
is to take that last step herself,
away . . .
so the child knows it is time,
that they are loved . . .
but trusted.
That now they must strengthen roots
for the dreams we fed, and nurtured.

We step away,
our faces proud,
hearts near bursting
and we swear we will not cry.
But when you step away dear child,
I will still be here.
Someday when I must do the same,
remind me of the words
I used to dry those tears.

❦ 10-Point System

Rate the pain on a scale of one to ten,
with one being almost nothing
and ten being the worst you've known,
and I always gawk at that question.
A normal day is *five* honey,
so nothing under a seven
really requires comment or notice.
But let me explain about 8, 9, and 10.
Eight is when you cannot move,
there is no *comfortable*,
and some part feels rotted
like a bad tooth.
Nine is when you try very hard
not to scream,
and try harder not to cry.
Ten is when you don't give a shit about pride,
and you cry,
and even cry out
and wish an 18-wheeler
would simply put you out of your misery.

❦ Glints In The Mirror

I never counted the looking glass as *friend*,
never looked for beauty
in eyes too gray for blue,
nor green enough for pretty.
When I stood before the glass
I saw a woman
who remembered not the dance,
but the longing to be lost
in music,
in strong arms,
in a dizzy world of no words.

While such was never my portion,
the hunger does not abate.
And when I am eighty,
will I still see those eyes of mine
silvered glints in the mirror
fool lights dancing in the meadow
that were never the ghost,
and ever the unspoken wish
of the young girl in the glass?

❧ Dignity, Honor & Grace

I. Dignity

Dignity is an old virtue,
mistaken at times for the formal manners of *regal*,
which isn't even a kissing cousin in concept,
as like to regal as cotton is to a peacock feather,
but something we all could possess were we so inclined.

Dignity is a humble garment,
worn best by those who don't know they possess it,
but well know the sight of it in another.
It can't be pretended, or feigned,
can't be purchased or purloined,
because it can't be separated from the spirit
for even an instant.

It is more like courage, akin to grace,
but an entity all its own.
Dignity is the deep of eye
possessed by those who have borne
the unbearable, who knew heinous loss,
or unspeakable outrage
yet carry themselves with spiritual calm.

Dignity is the voice that has known sorrow,
but lifts itself to laughter
when another is in need.

Dignity is carried beneath the skin,
by the old souls who walk in silent truth,
and do not need to keep time
with others who have long forgotten
if they ever truly knew
a reckoning of their own hearts,
and an acceptance of their lives.

II. HONOR

Honor is the second sister,
too oft mistaken for Pride,
but she is a quiet one, not much for self praise.
Honor is the gift of doing
what feels right to the soul,
not because it leads to something,
not because it is expected,
or because it is the pretty thing,
but because something within you requires it.

Honor is twinned with Valor,
but all twins are separate
no matter that they are mistaken for each other.
Honor is not about courage,
though they require each other to live.
Honor is knowing yourself
so well and so completely
that when it is needed,
you will act without thought,
and choose what is truest to your heart.

III. GRACE

Grace is the rarest of these fine three,
for she walks very lightly amongst us.
She is frequently seen with Dignity,
is the soft in the eyes of the hard pressed,
is the quiet of the tempestuous life,
and the one who knows
that each person must have a say.

Where grace has been,
her passing is noted.
The weary are a little less tired,
the callous are more inclined to seemly,
the heart-worn find a moment of succor,
and all these things are given
with open hands, not clenched fingers
to hold tight to the gift,
to make sure you know who gives.

Grace is Sunday's child,
the face of one who knows
just the words to lift a burden
if only for an instant.

Grace is the essence of a soul,
and her scent is unmistakable,
not a heady perfume
not cloying or oversweet,
just the subtle whiff of rain-washed air
after the arid heat
of too long a drought.

Dignity, Honor and Grace,
so rarely seen in our days,
almost never spoken of
or considered in a world of individuals
who have nearly forgotten
the necessary congress of humanity.

I will honor them where I find them,
and hold those precious few as dear,
and hope that someday I possess
these true riches of the soul.

❧ I Ain't Martha Stewart

My house is way past cluttered,
the cookies are not done,
my wrapping paper doesn't match
but I'm still having fun.
Martha Stewart would simply die,
if she could see this place
but I suspect that little witch
could never keep my pace.
I do not have a staff of 12
to get my kitchen neat,
chase dust bunnies from under the bed,
or make my house look sweet.
I do not have the breath or time
to think of *festive themes*
and she is just not my kind,
with her domestic schemes.
I simply do from can to can't,
have a list of will and will not's,
and I could give a good goddamn
if disarray gives her trots.
So Merry Christmas all dear friends,
and have a wondrous year,
I don't give a fig for *winter white*
there's no Martha Stewart here.

❧ Closure

I have learned to dread that word,
the reigning queen of pop psychology
thou shalt deal with thy dysfunction,
cast out your personal demons,
not be a downer for the world,
and do it PDQ
lest ye be regarded as *affected*.

There are things that need
more than two minutes of Dr. Phil,
when the soul and spirit
have been beaten down,
and "Get over it" is just stupid,
because in that rush to neatly tie
pretty bows on human misery
we can't reduce all suffering
to bite-sized sound bits
suitable for mass consumption.

In point of fact,
some people live their lives
chock full of real emotions,
of feelings that go beyond
the first layers of skin,
and they get involved,
because real life doesn't lend itself
to *neat as a pin* tidiness,
or something you can clear
with a paper towel and a light spray
of fresh pine cleanser.

Closure is a pretty dream
suitable for *made for TV* movies,
where it's all neatly wrapped by the end
into something Norman Rockwell painted.
What some of us do,
knowing that others cannot;
is live our lives in layers,
where each is seasoned
above and below
by what we tasted,
felt, and learned.

We may hold our ghosts
but that is a choice,
and a reminder that once
we held what they were.
It is unspeakable now to say,
"Leave, I am shut of you."

A cosmic *bon voyage*
is a cheap reward
for those who walked our lives
and never asked more
than the benediction of memory,
and the right to rest somewhere
beneath the stars and moon
they will never feel again.

ଘ THE ELDER BLOSSOM'S REQUEST

She is an old school blossom,
and well remembers the time,
when a man announced his intentions
with a two-step, and rhyme.
It doesn't really matter
that the choices she made,
left little time for dancing,
or games of charades.
But every so often she catches a song,
that hums to her spirit,
and sails her along
to wishes and hoping
and arms that are strong,
and gifts her with legs
that could dance all night long.
Those are the times
when she makes her request,
not fortune or riches,
or some lofty crest.
No, she is left longing
for a night flung with stars,
and glimmering planets
like Saturn or Mars,
and under that cloaking
of velveteen sky,
she longs to be dancing

with a gentleman shy,
who knows how to dip,
and tango and waltz,
who can kiss a fair wrist
all that sweet lovely schmaltz.

So if you are hearing
a nightingale call
perhaps you're just hearing
her heart, after all.

❧ FAULKNER'S HEAT

You can't catch it sitting calmly,
head full of easy, breezy thoughts,
no.
Heat must layer,
in general and specific,
the plump of the flesh
spongy with want
rising
raging
no I cannot think
yes I must be had,
yes it must be you,
and I want *fast* but make it *slow*
so I mew like a hungry kitten,
feeling only hot star-fire
filling my belly,
leaving a plump hollow,
not empty,
but not quite full.

A thousand fantasies not my own,
did nothing to cause this,
but a sudden awareness
that you knew
and sat with a bemused smile

as words licked at me,
touched,
tousled,
I am pure need,
vestal in a house of pleasures,
but I can't even guess
what you are thinking
or which touch
will turn you into sultry fire,
and make you unleash
the Faulkner's heat
onto a dizzy world
where flesh is king.

☙ Whisper Touching

Most read the words,
feel the hunger barely restrained,
witness the knowing
and think they have glimpsed
the all of me,
sexy woman
cocksure,
strong,
confident in the ways of pleasure.

You came gently,
cupped a chin,
saw the eyes I hide
beneath lashes,
and knew that there was only
half a woman there.
Worldly wise,
yes, I can pleasure a lover
embed the knowledge
of me into their flesh
so completely
that they miss

how very afraid I am
to open to their knowing.

I let them touch the skin,
shiver from small pleasures
but never have I given them
foothold
purchase
access to the inner self.
You speak softly
and I offer my secrets
spoken sadly
in near shame
eating the blame
that none have ever tried
to coax
from folded petals,
guilty that I have never given myself
completely to any lover . . .
because I don't know how.

You told me that the flower
will bloom lush and full
when a lover's lips
make a habit of kissing the petals,
and I laughed in fear of it,
this pleasure I do not know.
But you will never understand
the quiver that went through me,
when you stated all *matter of fact*
that when I felt your mouth on me
it would feel right
and natural,
just a logical progression
of the tasting,
the sampling,
the moment
I crave in my secret heart;
and smelted me
by suggesting I might possess

buried deep in folded woman flesh
the perfect drug you made
in one night
of whisper touching.

❧ Sourwood Hunger

Sourwood hunger is powerful strong,
the sweet that you crave
when the hours grow long,
the sticky sweet bliss
you can feel to the soul,
grown from love deeper
extracting its own toll.

Sourwood hunger,
a drizzle of you
when no other honey
will ever quite do,
it's dark and it's sweet
when spread on my skin
I shiver and quiver
and long to begin.

Sourwood hunger
is blazing inside,
the kiss that you left there
is something I hide.
When I pretend
that I really don't burn,
the sourwood hunger will surely return.

So feed me my darling,
the taste of your skin,
let me sip freely of what you begin,
taste what you've awakened
in my sweetest core . . .
know Sourwood hunger
like never before.

⌘ Lattice Wings

Spun of silk once,
ripe with dreams
wings are made without the seams,
made for flight, and made to soar,
I know I had some wings before.

Perhaps they were too often used,
though more then likely just abused
and so I kept my flying down,
keeping low, more to the ground.

You never fall too far that way,
at least that's what some people say.
Only . . .
wings do heal, to my surprise
you saw the flight dream in my eyes,
kept me close to warm my wings,
whispered low of softer things
and let me float when I was able
gifted me a kiss like sable.

Taught me once again to fly,
how could I not traverse your sky?
Now I flutter, not in fear
but hoping you will join me, dear.

⌘ Cold It Comes

Wind whistling through the disconnected soul
and the skin is a shabby shawl at best,
worthless for keeping the banshee at bay.
I am awake with words licking my eyes,
laughing as I try to nail them flush.
I am at odds with the brain
that repeats the sane and logical
like a mantra, or perhaps a prayer.

What is this twisting wild hurt,
what is the name for it after all?
Cold it comes to claim me,
and when I would run,
it pushes me down,
holds my wrists,
and says
"You are mortal."
Yet I spit in the eye of this demon,
and answer,
"I am only mortal when I die.
Until then, I *live*."

❧ SLEEPING WITH YOU

It's not about taking,
or skin hunger,
or rabid need,
so much as wanting to feel
your heartbeat,
wondering if you will hate
that I snore,
and hoping for that snagged ankle
that hauls me near.

It's about whether you will wake
in the cerulean dark,
watch me sleep,
and chase one bit of hair
that would devil my eyes.

So don't be alarmed
when I say. "Sleep with me."
It has less to do with lusting,
and more to do with simple trust,
and wanting you to be there.

❧ SEEKING WISDOM

The universe does not offer personal ads:
"Cosmic truth in search of open minded seeker,
contact Deity at . . . "

No short-cuts, or self-help books
that speak with the same tone
as the quietest voice we possess,
but frequently ignore,
distracted by louder sounds
with less significance.

We search for truth but do not trust
that we will know it,
so we look for glimmers
in the world outside that suggest
someone knows something we missed,
misread, or didn't understand.

It never once occurs
that *bliss* is a state that comes
only when you abandon the answers
someone else has given
to a life only you lived,
only you paid for,
and only you knew.

Why is a question for reporters.
But they do not live,
they only tell us how someone else did.
What we each need to learn
will never be found in black and white.
It is only glimpsed when we feel the bells,
the drums, the cadence
of a heart in tune at last
with what the rest of our life
has been saying.

☙ Honors Rendered

Coming to this place,
amidst the stone garden
in no way Zen,
to render the honors of a life,
shared hours,
traded words,
laughter now more a ghost
than you, dear one.

They blanket the surface
with unnatural green
so we will not see
the torn ground made ready
for this last billet,
and we will leave before
they lower you,
a curse and blessing both.

Part of me is grateful not to see,
part of me demands to know,
wanting to force myself
to fully render you these honors.
Taps is yours dear one,
this dark will not harm you,
but I came here to lay
those bits, and pieces, and dreams,
the heart moments,
the breathless wonders,
and yes the love,
to rest as well.

I force myself not to cry, but
I know the truth in the last note
of the bugle,
in the sounds the women make,
when roses are laid to metal.

There is no place here
to bury love . . .
there is only room for the part of you
life no longer requires.
Honors rendered,
and the last tears are for me,
knowing that the love
is something I must carry
until the pall they bear is my own.

But I was faithful,
and in the last,
gave you full measure, the honors rendered.

❧ Pop Rocks

Naturally, candy to some;
but to others
a unique recreational opportunity
for the truly discerning palate.

You doubt?

Well lean close for a minute,
while I pour a little on my tongue . . .
then kiss me quick and hard.

Ah . . . you're getting the idea.

Now just imagine a trail of that,
sprinkled here and there,
and what would happen
when a wet tongue swirled,
just so?

Ohhh . . . you are getting it!

I can see I have your . . . attention.
Yes, I believe you are thinking hard.

Now . . . Want to try a little kid stuff?
It's not just for breakfast anymore.

Snap.
Crackle.
. . .

❦ PHILADELPHIA, ART AND THE KID

Desi has her own way
of looking at things,
so you can understand why
the art museum made me . . . nervous?

She did not even try to hide
her utter contempt of Warhol
(*BRILLO BOXES????*)
And The Nude Descending The Stair
(*Mommy, that man NEVER saw a naked woman.*)

Even the Masters were not spared
her gimlet eye and tongue
(*Guess They didn't have Jenny Craig.*)

But truly her most shining moment came,
when an art-fart tried to make her understand
minimalism.
Desi listened politely,
nodded,
and then asked the art-fart
"But what did his mother do with the OTHER Crayons?"
And the silly biddy had no idea
that Desi was joking.

We escaped without injury.

I can't wait till she sees the Dada school . . .

❧ BETTER TO KNOW

Better to know where you stand
in the great scheme of things . . .
for when you don't
you may fall prey
to wistful imaginings,
and think you count
a lot more than you do,
and start wondering
Why NOT me?
instead of the usual
Not I.

Better to know
that I am not really the light
in a pair of loved eyes,
better to know
the moment you thought sacred
was just an occasion of regret.

Better to know
that you are just
a glimmer, not really a shine
and though it hurts in the well of you
it is always better to know
then to feed fodder to dreams
you should have left
back when the Bee Gees
were stars.

❧ NOT THESE BONES

The churchyard is silent witness
to every passing, great or bleak.
I have knelt in the remains of leaves,
breathed the moss as incense,
and traced fingers over chiseled words

wondering each time
what the seasons tasted like
to a shade long departed.
I saw the blossoms nursed by tears,
and wondered if they spoke for them,
and at last I knew the place too smug
for the rowdy likes of my passage.
So the wind shall have me,
tossed over the waves to cheat the gulls
one last time.
Do not look for a place,
or a neatly cut stone
to say that I stopped last there.
I will be the wind
that blows hair in your eyes,
or carries the smell of rain
in tiny swirls to your senses.
Do not look for me in the place of silence,
when I have forever lived this life
as a wind chime against the quiet.

✿ LANGUAGE LESSONS

Eskimo words challenge my tongue,
asking sweet contortions
and dazzling clicks,
while French offers a modest three words
for friend,
but only one means lover.
Somehow I knew I could laugh with you,
wet spot be damned,
enough a male to delight
in the Cheshire wench who asks to dance
under the solid weight of you,
eyes flashing,
lips soft,
toes curling in small circles.

So teach me this new language please,
and don't forget
the few thousand new words
that invoke the divine
with heated breath,
and slow articulations
while my hair flies wild
in my eyes . . . or yours.

❧ And I Do Fondly Love You

I heard you speaking for a heart,
your heart . . .
wondering what was different,
wondering why it felt
like golden velvet
folded unto itself.
You did not speak of partings,
but I felt it
in the way you joined to my skin,
listened like a fretful child
for the beat of my heart.
I said I would hold you
somewhere in my heart,
in days
or months
or years,
and wept when you said
I should not murder my seldom spoken dreams.
I could not
you could not
say a sort of farewell
without this touching.
You asked if I knew
what I had given you,
and yes dear one, I did.
I gave you safe harbor,

a touch you hungered for,
and I taught you
just how much was worth loving.
I did so knowing
this night would come.
So my sweet love,
go.
Regret will not wear your name,
and I will never wish
that we had never happened.
Doubt yourself.
Doubt the world.
But never doubt
what you are to me,
or that I so fondly love you.

⊗ About You

There is about you something defying all words,
a tang of more than your skin,
that I will never catch, nor seek to cage.
There is the wild of a raptor in your gaze,
something that can never be tamed,
sacrilege to think of, or try.
You are wood smoke,
and wisps of dreams half remembered,
You are the first splash of rain
in the too dry July,
You are the flash of the shooting star
that dazzles my mortal eyes,
You are the still of morning haze,
refusing to bow to the sun,
or give way to the bird song.
About you
there are the thousand unasked miracles
that can never be owned.
There is about you,

something more always
than meets the eye.
And always there is something
about you.

☙ Happy Father's Day

Love is not always what makes babies . . .
Love comes later,
after the awestruck look
the counting of toes,
the ear-splitting grin
at the first crowed "Daadaaaa!"
Tell me you ever saw a man
look the same way
when little miss all-of-three
grabs his knee, and hauls herself up
for the hug she deserves.
Or when the apple that didn't fall far
looks up at his dad with shining eyes
and wonders if he will ever stand so tall.
But whatever the alchemy
that turns any man
from male to something more,
I have seen this magic happen
and abracadabra always begins
with one word . . . "daddy."

☙ Mouth To A Kiss

When you talk of smoky Merlot,
wrapping soft tendrils to the senses,
and offer me a glass as dark as your eyes,
I am reminded of wine lingo,
and what they call "mouth" in a vintage.

Are you offering me wine,
something to make me go soft
or are you offering me
mouth to a kiss?

I am more like the Riesling,
sweet, fruity to dry
with no hidden puzzles or delights . . .
there is no mistaking my hue.

In my case, the cork says nothing,
or at least not enough.
The only way to know my flavor
is to taste,
so, my dear
shall I give you mouth to a kiss?

✿ PLEASURES

Something about the word
suggests satin and silk.
Whispers
like hair falling from pins
onto shoulders
creamy enough to bite.

Pleasures,
rich,
like fine velvet
that will leave marks
from the lightest finger touch.

You pleasure me
with looks
that rain warm on my skin,
color my cheeks,
and turn me like potter's clay
in your hands.
Firm,
they shape,

caress the detail
pinch softly,
and make the final form
that I will take.

I pleasure you
with soft sighs,
breathe in stitches,
and glow
amber gold,
honey gleaming
and it becomes all we are,
or have wished to be,
fingers joined,
bodies close held,
a personal beat between us,
overlaid heart to heart
in time.

Pleasure me, my love,
take, that I may give
all that is mine
yours now
in this swirl of color
this fragile skin,
this healing vessel
fueled by your love,
fired by passion
and emerging
from the kiln
as something rare,
and priceless.

❧ HEART OF MINE

Letting go of you
was hard for me, heart of mine,
so different from the man I first met
who did not feel worthy
good, kind or decent
because another love
had held you to an impossible yardstick
of not who you were,
but who she wished you would be.

And oh, my sweet,
how you pushed and pulled
and tried to shape yourself
like silly putty of the soul,
trying not to hurt when you proved
to be only mortal and human.
Loving you was easy,
so easy that I broke my own rules.

When I found myself wanting
more than I knew you could give,
I knew it was time
to gather my wits and heart,
make a neat bundle,
and give you the best chance I could.

God speed, heart of mine.
I will see your face in tonight's moon,
and pray that these tears
don't taste like yours,
but after all this time,
I know they will.

❧ Eating Cherries

Sultry night air,
clinging to skin
like wet gauze,
and I swear you could not offer
a morsel that would induce me to eat.

Then you say it.
Cherries.
Perfect.
Round.
Chilled.
So firm to the teeth,
then juicy sweet,
and you offer one to my lips . . .
no hands,
you murmur.
Just . . . your lips,
and maybe your tongue.

The game begun
I bite the first
as you look at my face,
into my eyes
in a smoldering way.
The next I rest on my tongue,
roll it softly
teasing myself,
teasing you
before again,
I bite down.
Sweet.

This time you hold it
and I nibble the juicy flesh
feeling it stain my lips
and start to trickle down.
You catch one drop on your finger,
and offer it to me . . .

as delicate as a kitten,
I lick
then suck softly on that finger,
never once letting my eyes close,
or drop.

"Want one?"
I ask, a voice rich and low,
then place a cherry firmly
between my teeth.
You close the distance,
and I know we are going to share
our first kiss
sweet with the taste
of firm dark cherries.
Your lips
firm on mine,
your hands wound in my hair,
and in the instant
the fruit is eaten
I want nothing more
than the taste of you.

ꕥ Rich Warm Broth

You can't feed gourmet fare
to a belly leaning against the backbone
when a touch would be just too much.
You have to go slow,
build the hunger up.

Try not to look too deep in the eyes,
as you spoon up the slow-cooked
rich, warm broth I need.
I don't want you to see my fingers shake,
don't want you to know how keen the need,
as your arms close slowly around me.

The shaking will abate,
just let me sip slow,
become familiar with the feel,
till the growling slides lower than my belly.
I am not so dizzy that I cannot feel
your hands starting to move on me.

The warm grows from the inside out,
this *half-starved* losing the impulse to grab,
to gorge while the getting is good.
Then I am a woman again,
the dozing she-being
curled to your flesh,
ripe for your taking,
sweet singer who remembers the words
she lost when music stopped touching her skin.

☙ MISS BETTER THAN NOTHING

They chose to be with you, right?
After a fashion.
I was Miss *Better Than Nothing*
a few times too many.
When they had tried all my friends,
wasted their money and conversation
and the choice was me,
or going home alone,
well . . . I won the toss.

But that didn't make me what they wanted,
didn't make them hungry
for any special part of me.
I was a generic female.
Tits . . . two.
Cleft . . . yes.
Better than a night of solitary pleasure,
but that didn't make it *me*
they desired.

That was long ago.
But the memory of nights
when they didn't even know my name
is burnt into me.
You wonder how I can feel
the way I do,
when "better than nothing"
wasn't "nothing,"
but it sure as hell
wasn't much.

✿ HARD CASE

Little girl,
I have had a life,
not the worst,
not looking for medals,
or pity,
wouldn't change a thing.
There is no box to check
that asks if your family
was dysfunctional,
gives credits for surviving rape,
or if your folks thought a belt
would improve you as a person.
They do not care
that love was some shiny dream
you could not bring yourself
to hope for,
or that you wept away
the darkest part of any night.
No matter what you are handed,
the choice is yours
to live, and win
or to let them turn you
into their kind of ugly.
So you hold onto whatever is *you*.

They can hurt the body,
they can make you scream,
and pray for death,
but they can only
rape the very heart of you,
if you *let* it happen.

໕ No Hearts, No Flowers

It happens every year,
when I see the first fat red heart,
cupids, lace doilies.
Oh god.
Cold.
Ice cold shoots through me.
Hospital smells,
swabs,
a victim kit
instead of a valentine.

It will be 23 years
since an innocence I didn't know
I even possessed
was ripped from me.
Do I even remember what they looked like?
How many,
did I fight,
did I scream,
(did I like it)?
I remember,
until the numb is all through me.
I live it again,
make myself feel
what they did.

God and I parted ways
for quite a while then.
For two years,

I could not stand to be touched
without wanting to scream
or cringe.
I grew back my soul,
the part they could not kill,
but every February
the cold comes back.

I remember sitting in the ER
while they bagged my panties.
I could see
valentines everywhere
and knew there would never be
another Valentine's day for me,
no matter how long I lived.

ℭℜ KLINGON LOVE

No, not my usual flavor or speed,
I am given more to shades of *shy*
when it comes to man and woman,
the awareness of the two.
But when the moon is just so
and the stars are right,
I want to be a **Klingon**.

I mean it . . .
daggers strapped across my breast,
a swagger that spells danger,
and any male who looks my way
had better mean business,
better be brave,
because the duel is just foreplay.
And you know that whatever follows,
will involve biting,
and screaming.
If you think you have war wounds now,

just wait till you see what you get
when I morph into **Klingon**.

When *act of love*, and *act of war*
are words for the same thing,
you better want me bad . . .
because honey, that kiss will cost you.
No time for sissy girls like Xena, no.
I am woman.
I am scary.
I am **Klingon!**
You better not retreat once you start,
because the weak are hunted down,
and devoured . . .

⌘ WHEN CHARLES MET DESIREE

I remember the first time
you held her
your eyes so soft
face astonished
and tender
my god, so gentle.
She barely filled your arms,
and she wriggled,
yawned
and slept there
as if she knew
that your heart
had just leapt into her tiny hands.
Fourteen years have passed,
and I see *that* look steal into your eyes
when she flies to your arms
covers you with kisses,
and calls you that magic name
you have grown to own.
It does not matter
that you had to make room

in that man's heart,
or that at times I know
she is the shining star
of your soul, not I.
It only matters
that on that day
when you feasted your eyes,
unable to believe
she was ours,
that I watched pure love
born
as you held your girl
for the very first time;
that you had no words
to catch
the way she caught your heart,
the first time I saw
the *daddy* in you.

☙ Sweet Tea Spring Infusion

Rain-washed breeze
shook the cherry,
the apple,
and the peach,
stole the perfume
from countless blooms
to make a new scent
never bottled or captured.

The old-eyed souls had best
stick to their taters,
because this little woman
has a mason jar of cold, sweet tea,
a silk kite that is shamelessly pretty,
and is inclined to just breathe
the yellow pollen air.

So if you are creaking in your bones,
barely survived this winter's cold,
if you are caught in the battle for balance
all but flattened by the fight
I will prescribe my solution
with not the merest qualm.

You're needing a lick of lilac,
a large dose of Spring in bloom,
and even if that heart swears
it can never feel the sweet benediction of warm,
sit with me beneath the blossoms,
and wait for the first strong breeze
to cover you with petal kisses.
Sip from the jar of honey-sweet tea,
then tell me
you've grown too old for Spring
and the infusion of life to the senses.

❧ CONVERSATIONS WITH THE UNCONVENTIONALLY KINDRED

You never know what to expect
when the talk waxes from poetic
to profound,
when it feels like a soul
is searching for something elusive.
I am not so much a shoulder,
but just the echo
of the words in the well
of a heart gone to disquiet.

Asking questions not of me,
but more a query of God . . .
trying to get the wording right
so there is no chance
of miscommunication.
You cannot offer heart's ease

to a soul that deems itself unworthy in one breath,
yet has the courage to labor over the questions.

I am no more than the still pond,
and each stone tossed
makes a ripple of circular tension.
Observe that the water always
returns to still,
but do not think you have not made a mark.
The last ripple settles to calm . . .
but still there is below the surface
the cairn you built,
the dreams you spilled,
and the music you shared,
to mark the place where you spoke
your conversations
with the unconventionally kindred.

❧ Gazing At Goya
(One Part)

I stood in disbelief,
as the skin lost to ages
shimmered with inner light,
as eyes closed long ago by time
looked into my own,
shared soft secrets
that perhaps they had whispered
to the artist.

Though he held his tongue,
no one could still his brush,
so he painted the heart of them
in rich oils
for us to wonder at
and secretly wish
that we had the fire
one painter had seen,

and captured
because it spoke to him
the words of a muse,
and light of a soul,
until the very skin of you
begged to be painted
as only Goya could have done.

ᛒ Moon Ridge

When the sun falls behind
the blue shadowed hills,
the heat of day departs.
Without a word,
you hunt out kindling
and some dry logs for a fire.

Dinner done, I watch the sky deepen
to an impossible violet
spangled with starlight,
glazed by the Milky Way
and know that I am waiting.

But I need more than the view
through glass.
When you have a gentle blaze started,
I inhale the sweet smell of pine and pear wood.
We go to the veranda to scan the sky
and it is enough to be a whisper apart,
my head against your shoulder.

Ah . . . there.
A cool breeze fills the hollow,
unasked, your arms enfold me,
lips warm against my ear.
"You never tire of it, do you?"
There seems so much more to that question
than whether I will always love
the red September moon

bracketed by cedar and oak,
or this house we made together,
or those moments tucked in your arms
under flannel sheets.
You are asking
if I will always love the Ridge,
always love you?

I pour all the words
into one kiss as the moon quietly climbs
offers sweet radiance
and blissful benediction
to two lovers
who made hearts into home,
home into life . . .
and life into this house
set in the hollow
as the moon casts its glow
over the Ridge.

☙ FEELS LIKE SIX

Twelve degrees outside
and they say it feels like six,
something to do with wind-chill.
But I am wrapped in wool shawl,
feet in socks,
fingers still cold
after a night run,
listening to the fevered tossing
of one unhappy little girl.
Feels like six,
but I feel old and young
and nowhere near the island of sleep.
I am tasting the blues
that will not play,
planning a day of condolence.
So sad the news,

fore and aft.
We knew that Marion
would go soon,
spoke of it just this week.
But Michael was still not old
and his wife who called him
a silly man,
mourns him with silence.
She will wear basic black
her wedding ring,
and try not to look
like she lost the best friend
she never knew she had.
The condolences
will fall like dry snow,
and even if it warms,
it will feel like six.
Two a.m. and I am not alone
in my thinking
that life is too many seasons
with too few days,
and no one
ever really gets to say goodbye . . .

○₰ Midnight Shift, Angel Patrol

Just a routine drive-by,
searching for the wayside hearts,
the quiet ones who sigh deep,
but have given up hope
that any of the world cares
about their grief
their hurt
or the painful silence of their lives.

The job is to reach out,
try to erase the idea
they are just a number,

no matter what the world taught them.
You don't care about the odds,
or the fact that this job can seem futile.
You're on the Angel Patrol
and you are needed
because there are precious few angels.

You aren't cold fusion,
the key to world peace,
or the answer to an age-old bane.
You're just someone who cares enough
to touch one soul
and say, "You count,"
or "I'm sorry,"
or "Let me help you with that,"
so the spirit can catch a breather.

Our job is to get there
before the eyes go flat,
before the last spark sputters out.
They may not thank you,
they may walk away
and never care you were there.
But they're on their feet,
not their knees anymore,
and that means it worked.

The working hours are crap,
there's no pay that most would count,
and the one thing you can rely on
is job security because brother . . .
they are *everywhere.*

But you can make a tiny difference,
not spit in the ocean,
just one small thing
that no one else thought to do.
The angel patrol
is on the prowl
in the black night hours
or the desperate silence of day.

Look Clarence,
there's another one.
Time for me to earn some wings.

❧ AUNT ANNA'S KITCHEN

Anna Married Tony . . .
that part I knew,
rocked the family
back in the 40's
because he was something else
and we were Czech,
and that was interracial back then.

They had two boys,
bought a house in Bayonne,
Tony died
not long after I was born,
leaving Anna alone.

She was young when it happened,
probably could have found another guy
but you always got the feeling
that he was still around,
and she spoke of him
all those years later.
Her eyes would look off,
she would tap a cigarette ash,
sip her coffee
and say his name like
she'd just talked to him a few minutes before.

I never thought it strange
sitting there with her,
never wondered where he was,
always thought maybe I had missed him
leaving for work,
and part of me knew he was gone,
but in Anna's kitchen,

she was just a lady waiting for her fella
and teaching a niece the secrets
of kolachy or fresh turkey soup.

She waited a lifetime for that man,
and the call just came.
I guess Tony picked her up,
her beautiful, dark-haired lover
with the dago eyes
finally came to get his girl.
I'm happy for Anna,
but I'll miss her just the same . . .

For love,
for cookie dough,
for cups of sweet coffee,
for talking to me like I was smart
and loving me, not just because I was
my dad's kid.

Goodbye Anna.
Uncle Tony, take good care of her,
make it worth her wait, okay?

✿ SOUL COCOA

If I could,
I would surprise you
with a steaming mug of hot chocolate
so you would forgive me
for waking you at this indecent hour.
Nearly 4 a.m.,
too early to be late,
too late to be early,
flooded with words
choked with emotions
that *moody* just doesn't cover.

Sister,
have you ever looked hard

at the almost full moon
just a sliver short
and longed for arms
to wrap you close
stroke your hair,
and tell you
that the dawn will make it all
somehow warm again?

Feed me chocolate,
dark, rich cocoa from Holland,
marshmallows to melted froth
steamy with sweetness.
Put mittens on my chilled soul
and forgive me
for waking you
when you were sleeping warm.

☙ FULL BODY KISSING

Not the first kiss . . .
more like a tasting of wine
you swirl on your tongue,
softly given so no one is shaken,
but that kiss will tell you
if any of the rest will follow.

The arms go round shoulders and waist,
and the next kiss you will feel
through every layer of clothing,
as one tries to slip beneath the defenses,
the moment of tense
to comfort and release,
and *God* yes, you may.

The legs open first to the press of a knee,
and when you feel the push of want,
the stamp of desire,
you roll and crest and angle for more,

because lip to lip is close,
but not near close enough.

I want to feel your whole body kissing mine,
while your mouth does slow, lovely things
and mine is caught between
you, and I and the hard place
I want to feel to my last cell.

Now . . . about the kiss you promised?

❧ Consummation, Considered

Every step of this dance
is lace filigree held to light
examined for flaws,
until we are nearly toe to toe,
one breath from a kiss,
and all I need do
is close the distance
from me to we . . .
and do so without the tremble.

It was easier to bare my soul,
to show every scar I carry,
then to be naked
before your eyes.
Can I be the woman,
the wet,
the wonder you have dreamed?
Can my skin be what you wish,
the scars and puckers
near enough to fill you?

We have danced, and dipped,
tango to lambada,
your hands pulling me
hip to hip,
your breath so close to my ear,
and nothing I have seen

in these weeks and months
scared me near as much
as my reflection
in your confessional eyes.

ଊ A Time For Poetry

When you have filled the days and nights
with *had to*, and *have to*,
when you labored for love or money,
the *needed* or *wished for*,
when all this is counted and culled,
something inside may call for words
to speak of deeper things.

The voice you did not know you had
will sing low . . .
strummed to the resonance
of misted moon or crystal clarity,
a craving for some flow and form
you never knew,
but suddenly cannot stem.

A time comes for poetry,
though it is not rocket science,
nor an answer to any question
the wise may long ponder,
or the discordant debate.

A time comes for poetry
when you would rather float
with the hummingbird,
or sashay with the bumblebee
than explain to an unbelieving world
that stars have earned their right to dance.

❧ THE STARS ABOVE ME
(9-11 poem)

Tonight the sky was flat,
the night air too quiet,
and I scanned the deep, blue velvet,
remembering the nights
I cursed the false blinking lights
that crisscrossed the heavens.

Without them,
the stars would seem brighter,
I thought.
But tonight my wish came true,
and it seemed there were holes
where something should have been
and I took no joy in my silent sky.

All at once,
the things I thought as torment
were as nothing . . .
less than nothing.
I saw the full lot empty,
and the empty lot full,
and though I can see
what the madmen did,
the print of their act is everywhere.

In the market,
people looked for my eyes,
wanted nodding assurances,
even from me, a stranger,
that our world still was,
despite the words and pictures,
despite the fear.
All day I heard happy shouts . . .
this one was late for work,
that one had the flu,
and one man's daughter

had a hangover
that he is still thanking God for.

But I knew as I drove home
that my world had changed.
I stared at the stars
little changed since our dawning,
shining like they did
yesterday's yesterday.
I know there is a God,
I know there is mercy,
I know the tears will fill an ocean,
and still I am fool enough
to pray for peace,
as the stars shine above me.

☙ Talking To My Belly

When I first felt the new of you,
solid,
growing,
it seemed only natural
to start a conversation,
to explain why I laughed and cried
at things you could not yet see.
You had no name,
no features I could trace . . .
but you became a little more real
as you grew quietly.
Not one for somersaults,
you moved only three times
the whole eight months inside me.
So when you arrived,
you were not quite a stranger
to momma's voice.
I fell in love slowly,
handled you like rare glass,
always afraid I would slip,

terrified I would do lasting harm.
But I still talked to you,
when all you could do
was smile at my babble.
One day when the woman at the market
said in annoyance,
"She doesn't understand a word, you know,"
I smiled back and answered,
"Oh, but one day she will."
Today changing my clothes,
I saw the marks you left,
ghost trails across my belly,
and it did not bother me to see them.
They were just proof
that you had lived there,
left your mark, dear one,
on my body,
as deeply as you have
on my heart.
If life has been insane,
please never forget
that you are loved,
and cherished
and it was an honor
to be the first place
you called home.

☙ WITHOUT A WORD
(9-11 poem)

He came home,
shell-shocked,
hollow-eyed like me.
We talked,
numb words falling
like the two buildings
and all those lives.

We went upstairs
took off our clothes
and came together
without a word;
not lust,
not desire,
not making love,
not fucking;
maybe just a need to feel something
that did not taste of ash,
or feel like blood;
maybe just an act of defiance
played with bodies
that said
without spoken words,
I am not dead
you are not dead
You **MISSED US,** you bastards.
Without a word.

ᛰ Soon

Soon.
Four letters, two of them the same,
but when you said it to me
last black-velvet midnight
moving toward blue,
the shiver of electric need,
copper tasting,
nerve tangling,
sense jangling,
removed every last bone in my body.

"When?" would have been a fine question,
but "Now" was the answer I craved.
Soon.
Sexy little "s,"
looping around me like your arms

and hauling me in
for the exquisite tang
of your goodnight kiss,
and the very last letter in *yes*.
So I'll make it easy for you.
When *soon* arrives
the answer is *yes*.
Full body cast,
domestic chaos aside,
emotional roller coasters be damned,
the answer is *yes*.

⌘ WANT

Forget the ladylike decorum,
the pinky extended for one tiny sip
of warm tea from perfect porcelain.
Clear the table
with one swipe of that arm,
and lift me there,
forget the skirt,
forget the wisp of silk,
don't let one thing
stand between us
because right now
hunger just got your name
and I want you
like the desert parch
longs to sip that first
fat drop of spring rain,
this sort of crazy
doesn't give me room
to even pretend to be a lady.

❧ HALF A LOAF

Better than none, they say.
Better than hungry,
just . . . half hungry.
So we tell ourselves
that half a touch,
half a kiss,
half a life will do . . .
fill the moments, hours, days
with half truths
and lie
and say oh, no,
I don't need more,
when all the while
our soul is trying to escape
because half starved
isn't near enough.
I want to be worth
everything you've got,
want a moment without me
to be a waste of your precious time.
If I must be half a lover,
I'll take the end
with brain enough
to know that half
will never fill the belly
of this too long hungry heart.

❧ IN YOUR DREAMS

In your dreams
I was something shining,
warm and soft,
sweet to the kiss,
and tender to the touch.

In your dreams
I was beloved,
all you could wish,
gentle muse crowned
with the splendor of your care.

In your dreams
I was not to be touched,
though we both know
I am not so holy;
all too human.

In your dreams
I became occasion of sin,
despite the heart
that wept against such a word,
and now my touch is sullied.

I will not be the bait of suffering.
I will not lead you more astray.
I will not be seed corn to nightmares,
even if it means all I can be,
is in your dreams.

✥ Pale Shades Of Tears

I spoke of you by the half moon,
said the words I bury deep
to a kindred soul,
said I saw you dancing in the stars,
too true to a telling to bear,
and I will cry
not one tear before I must.
I wish that loving you
had been my choosing,
instead of something
that took me one night
beneath a moon more full
than this heart could be.

The price I must pay
is knowing I will see the half moon,
know it does not shine on you,
knowing it will fade, eclipsed
and still I must be
stronger than I wish.
Better you do not know
the silver of my tears.
Better you never feel
the colors you strike.
It was my fate to find you,
to read your leaves,
to breathe your scent
after the rain,
and to lose you
to a half-moon night,
when you could not resist
the songs I do not remember,
but your soul will never forget.

○₰ What May Come Of You

I already know my lips
will part like ripe apricots
against the merest touch.
So if you tarry a moment
when first we kiss,
you have been warned, I'd say.

Your hands go to my spine
to finger-play a tender touch
just before I fall into your eyes
arms wide open
to the very sweet of you.

I make no promises,
no rash vows of eternal perfection,
nor even a glimpse of what I feel

stirring,
moving,
forming in my deepest self.
No,
I do not know what will come of you,
save that I am already
trembling,
incandescent,
aflutter
with what may come of me
when at last I touch you
for the very first always.

☙ SCATTERED

I will make fine confetti of what we were,
glints, colors, and shine
uniform shapes for the wind to carry
when I sweep out this heart again.

Rose petals are fine for potpourri,
but dried, fall like stones
and are brittle edged,
lost for good and all to flight
they cling like burrs
when we would lose them
once the scent has gone.

Your voice fed the hungered heart,
tended tiny ember to flare.
Again I sit consumed,
wishing longing was not a place
where my name is so well known,
wishing the need would be as smoke.
You my love
are not a ghost to my nights,
but still fresh enough
for me to taste and savor.

I will scatter the ashes again,
chant like a Sybil lost to dream.
I will blink against the grit
when my still beating heart demands
that you are anything but over.

❧ Decoration Day

Once, the ladies came young and old,
some dressed in modest best,
others wearing the black
that was their silent way
to claim solitude,
or convey honor to those
made sacred to time.

The children came to clear the weeds,
small places cluttered with winter debris,
sometimes pausing to trace fingers over granite,
and wonder what the face of their father
might have felt like in their hands.

Solemn, but not sad exactly,
a way of counting the fallen,
whispering that you were not in vain.
Even the ones who's kin had faded
were given attention on Decoration Day.

If the ghosts shared the picnics,
tasting lemonade on bygone tongues,
or just reveled in being a part
of the world they left, who could say?
The world has turned much
since a churchyard was a place of quiet peace,
given over one day each year not to dread,
but inclusion in the life they knew.

I wonder how it was to be a woman,
knowing life had gone on
but knowing this one day she was allowed

to give memory, and respect, and love
to a man she lost to time and living
on the sweet late spring occasion
they called Decoration Day.

Note: Decoration Day became Memorial Day.

ଔ Bitch On Wheels

Just got done sucking the marrow
from your latest victim, I see.
You live your life in words,
but fear the sunlight
like a vampire,
because the dim light
is much more flattering.

I watched you hunt another one,
knock it to the ground like a gazelle,
and swipe with your claws
to spill its guts.
How dare you make so much of yourself,
you two-bit whore,
you vicious little viper,
with nothing to offer a world
but venom and disdain?

Get a life.
Try to live as if you had one,
and leave alone the weaker ones
who are too gentle
to believe those such as you
could really exist.

And if you truly insist on playing
that *queen of death* role,
don't be surprised
if someone tries to stake you,
fills your mouth with garlic,

and hauls your bony ass
into the bright light of day.

⌘ ONCE UPON A MICKEY D'S CHRISTMAS

The lines were out the door,
mall-based fast food
the day after Thanksgiving.
The only job I could muster
in an economy
where only the yuppies won.
Who could think of Christmas
when the student loan folks
were not caring
that a minimum wage gig
was the best I could get?
"No stupid . . . extra cheese,
no onion . . ."
and where do they find
these morons?
"Thank you ma'am
You have a nice day . . ."
But the kids were all dressed
in their holiday best,
dancing from one foot to the other
yelling, "When do we get to see Santa?"
Halfway back,
I saw a spot where one small girl stood,
in a green, velvet dress,
a sweet face peeping out
from behind her father.
As they got closer,
I saw her whole face,
heard the comments
all around her
that she could not have missed
if she tried.

"Did you see that?
Man . . . messed up!
Was it an accident,
or was she born that way?"
Her smile did not falter,
but I watched her daddy's face
fade to grim,
because all he saw was his angel.
It was their turn at last,
and I turned on the wattage to a smile,
"Hi little lady, you ready to see Santa?"
and she bubbled off her list,
glowing and proud.
Suddenly all I saw
was her daddy's angel.
I reached over that counter,
gave her a hug,
and told her I bet
the Big Guy would remember.
Her father paid for the food,
and told his daughter to find them a table.
He looked at me,
and his eyes were wet.
I just smiled again,
and said
"Merry Christmas, sir."
Suddenly the student loans didn't matter,
and minimum wage wasn't so bad.
I have carried that little girl's smile
in my heart every Christmas since,
when I get to feeling low
and wonder if everything about Christmas
isn't just a scam.
But if she could smile,
who am I
to give less to a season of joy?

❧ Heart Triage

We call it
meatball surgery of the soul,
no time for little niceties
when the patient can handle maybe an hour
of cutting,
but not two.
My job is to look fast and hard,
they are ALL walking wounded,
cull the bad from worse,
work the odds,
and decide who is just alive enough
to save,
versus the ones
who will only take time,
plasma,
then give up the ghost.

Death is waiting casually,
reading *Rolling Stone*,
looking bored.
He knows he will get his quota,
and the only question
is his guess about who
I will fight for . . .
who I will try to finesse away,
while he is sipping
a double dark espresso.

Live or die,
makes no mind.
Eventually he gets all the chips,
but I am honor bound
to make him wait,
and that is just the breaks
on the heart triage.

❧ Pickett's Field By Moonlight

Cool that night,
blessed with a fat, white moon
that silvered every rock and stone,
a walk seemed a suitable thing,
save for the forgotten thought
of what this place once was.
The rational mind says
that thousands who died
more than a hundred years before
left nothing but bones
that were neatly buried.
Naught to fear,
just a moonlit stroll.
When the tiny hairs danced
on the back of my neck,
I called it cold.
When the bare, mown field
seemed anything but empty,
I called it imagination.
When the light danced oddly,
I called it a trick of the moon.
I could neatly explain all,
save the crushing grief
that ate at my soul
as I stood there in silver light.
No kin of mine fell,
no blood of my line spilled,
and yet I felt it . . .
loss, and pain, and the final passing
of too many mortal souls
in far too little time.
All this I felt
in the haunted church
we call Gettysburg.
I could not help but carry those ghosts
home in my heart.

❧ From Where We Came

Life writes on us,
like paper, thick rich vellum,
calligraphy with raised letter perfection . . .
writes on us like a brick wall
the sloppy testimony of graffiti,
illumination unimagined
shouting the truth of a life.
Every word is colored
from where you came,
every letter shaped with a hand
that knew kisses, or slaps,
paper cuts, gouges or slashes,
maybe the soft reality
of another pressing love
through skin and pores.
Life writes on us,
tears to watercolor blurring,
scars or marks,
tattoos just a way of choosing,
what blooms on our skin,
what shows of our travels,
the ones who got beneath our skin
and left the markers all too well known
to remind us,
from where we came.

❧ Reaching For Your Deep

Simple minded I can be,
but straight forward in approach.
I reach for your face with both hands,
feel the ripples gone to rage,
every hurt you never healed,

every acid etching
that you have robed with time.

A kiss cannot quench your all,
a touch cannot ease a life of withdrawal
folding yourself into origami
shapes to menace the dark things
that gibber and caper,
seek to eat you before dawn.

I would come to your bed,
not as a carnal being
but one who blankets you
from the left-behinds,
the accusing eyes,
the voices too shrill to fade.

I would reach for your deep
with both hands,
whispering soft words that mean only
that someone was with you at dawn
warding off the petty demons;
trying to shield you
from the hurt you wear
like skin.

ೞ A Bear For Yumi

I read the words of loss and anguish
so keen they made me tear,
a small lady, distant now
eating her grief like ground glass,
trying to keep a heart beating
with an emptiness nothing can fill.

My daughter saw the tears
and said, "Momma . . .
if you loaned me a few dollars
I could make her a bear,
dress it in Marine blue,

and make sure the bear was soft,
someone she could hold,
or even hug.
We could call him Tony.
I know it's not the same, momma,
I know a bear will never be
all she is missing,
and I know she will always miss him,
but sometimes it helps
to have a place to put your love."

So today we will go,
make a bear for Yumi,
and dress it in Marine Blue.
It may never fill her arms,
or her heart,
but at least she will have
a soft, warm place
to put her love.

And we'll name him Tony.

☙ Haiku For A Heart

Perhaps the issue is not word choice,
but rather that you are caught
trying to fit too much
in too tight a pattern . . .
something we never managed to define.

There was never a name for this,
there was only marvel and delight
when outstretched hand met
hand held out,
fingers laced,
and moments melted like soft butter
on a warm tongue.

So you decided to grant it all
the dignity of a form . . .

nothing so grand as a sonnet,
hoping eastern simplicity
would somehow make it fit
a shape you could give name to.

I sit and watch,
knowing it is futile,
for the Muse may pen a thousand poems,
but never will she explain
that everything we are
can never fit in the bare walls
of a haiku for a heart.

௸ Too Good At Goodbye

Wow.
That almost didn't hurt at all,
save for the skin
that came off when you yanked
hard,
just to make sure you got it all . . .
to make sure I got the point.

I was flinching for a while,
truth told . . .
wondered when it would come,
intellectually pondered
what reason you would choose;
the ever popular,
"Just one of those things,"
or the less honest
but kinder, "I did not mean to hurt you."

I am too damned good at goodbye . . .
So I sniff the wind for that first scent;
sweat, nerves, or just cologne
too long in a bottle.
I know it's coming like flowers
you wish were never sent,

with a card that says
that same old thing,
"You're wonderful lady,
just not *my* wonderful."

❧ Adventures At The Green Grocer

You would enjoy the royal of eggplant,
perusing the peaches,
the lackadaisical of the leeks,
the high gloss of cucumbers,
while I am seduced by cherries,
involved with onions,
and pondering the potatoes on my list.

Dill, you demand,
with a voice that suggests
only a heathen would settle for dry.

I am bemused by the singular authority,
that says only butter will do
for a portabella sauté,
with razor-sliced garlic
to spank the lamb into shape.

Off I go to the green grocer . . .
a solitary pleasure I steal,
knowing you will be with me,
eyeing the asparagus,
checking the peppers,
and suspicious of the tomatoes
that seem too deftly shaped
to have the real flavor
of something wild from a vine.

Some may seek your bed,
eye you with carnal delight . . .

But I just want to rattle your cookware,
make a fine mess in your kitchen,

and watch your eyes
as you take that first taste
of cooking, my way.

❧ THE DAFT DEGREE OF THE CROCUS

Spring is not far behind
the impatient splash of the crocus.
Even daffodils have a certain wisdom,
but the crocus will always show up
ready to start the party
when Winter has not yet rolled away.

They shiver in their Sunday best,
and maybe even shrivel,
history, before the stately tulip
steps grandly into warmer air.
But silly or not,
it is the crocus,
humble and low to the ground
that gives Spring her wake-up call.

So maybe it doesn't play it safe,
and maybe it doesn't play it smart.
But it has guts
for such a little flower.

❧ NO SEASON OF REGRET

I want between us, come what may,
no season of regret,
no mauve shading of pathos
to color the trail of what has been.
We found each other with purpose,
touched the soft clay and sore places,
balmed the hurts that others left

and now must learn to forgive ourselves
for all that was less than perfect.

I want no tears to streak the page,
or leave you as tomorrow's victim.
Pay the debts you must,
and never try to hold more than you can,
be it love, or sunlight streaming through fingers.
I was not the Spring you thought,
just the most glorious Autumn
you ever owned,
and I will never wish we had not been.

There is healing found
in the embrace of spirit,
soft tendrils tracing out
one heartbeat at a time.
I beg you not to ever wish
for more than could have been.
If I was not the bird call
on a day of budding trees,
at least I was the sunlight on the tulipwood
your eyes might never have seen.

I will not have between us
a season of regret.

✂ FOLDING THE FLAG

I watched as hands
made precise movements,
made simple cloth
take razor edging,
and knew someday
I would have to fold the flag
of all you were
as they had done.

But they did not know you,
so I cannot keep my hands

quite as steady,
cannot keep my eyes so level . . .
and when I fold your flag
it will not be so neatly
because I know I will pause,
touch the cloth
a hundred times,
and think of you with love.

I honor you no less
but I cannot fold your flag
quite as they did,
for to me
you were not a stranger.

ᛰ The Show Of Hands

I am suddenly wordless, shy
wrapped softly in a sheet,
waiting for you to close the distance,
hair long and loose
providing cover and camouflage,
the tender in me
fluttering like Luna moths
just below the surface.

You watch my eyes for the mercurial mural,
changing from dull gray
to shades of green,
pupil larger,
as I reach for composure
while I casually let fall the cloth,
trying not to color,
so aware of the velvet in your look.

I beckon with the movement of my hands.
They trace the skin, lines of smooth,
polish flesh so softly pale,
hands to my breasts

not to conceal,
but to offer you a place to taste,
a moment of pause
before you traverse my body,
glowing with you again.

My hands trace the woman curve of hip,
frame the down at the delta.
I offer what is mine,
and all this you watch with eyes
so warm to the wet
that I am not long left alone
for the simple show of hands
you evoke in me.

℘ GRIEF

I object to such a small word,
having the power
to slide into my heart
stiletto bright;
making me bleed
sharp until I taste the copper
of tears I tried to stem.

I hate that grief can take on a face
that I can not touch
with more than words.
Damned small word
to make me rock
keen, and reach for you
where there is just a shadow.

❧ Magnolia Skin

I wish you could have tasted
the sweet breath of white magnolia,
waxy, velvet petals
heady in scent ready to open
under the slip of your touch,
parting to the nuzzle
so willing to spill the sweet,
brush me close enough
to bruise the lips,
smooth the skin,
and cover the distance
between all you wish,
and all I dream of flowers
you are meant to know.

❧ King Stone

This is the place of the old ones,
where kings are blessed or broken,
where the young may challenge,
where the seasoned may defend,
or if the time is come
may lay aside the mantle
lie down in pomp and dignity
and give up his breath
for the good of the clan.

I watch from the ring of stone,
tears barely contained
reading your eyes,
afraid you have chosen
what I cannot bear to watch.
Not your lady wife,
not the one who bore your seed,
just one who knew you best

as a man without crown or glory.
While you have not said the words,
I see the King Stone in your eyes.

The best of men do not kill themselves,
but you would give your blood
back to the Mother who blessed you,
let your heart go still in your breast
for no other reason,
than it is your time.
I feel the life in you,
surging and tangible,
but you will not believe,
or perhaps are just too weary
to stand another challenge
to all you are.

So if I love you as I do,
I must honor your choosing,
stand with the others
while you give one last time
to the good of your people.
I just do not know
how I will not cry out,
how to let go the man of you
so you can give what you will
to the hard cold flat of the King Stone
in one last blaze of glory.

⌘ Seducing Onions

I woke as you did,
some minutes before gray dawn,
coaxed the fire from the embers,
brewed coffee for the sunrise,
and thought of you
as I rough-cut the onions

for the wild-rice dish
you might just like.

Between coffee sips,
using breath to bring
dry to new wood,
I am seducing onions,
can feel your eyes
as I take them from innocent white,
to succulent translucence,
then golden brown delicacy.

Dawn crept in on the lake mist.
In that first light
I could see her sleeping still,
her face soft, her sweet lips
the calm of the child
I watched grow these years.
Thirteen seems a world away.
I wonder if I knew such calm
when I slept so young.

So I will pen letters,
from this lake by the pines
and you will begin your day,
sip at coffee
and wonder again
why all you could smell
when first you woke
was the simple seduction of onions.

☙ A Better Mousetrap

Just words . . . only words
spent by each in their way
dropped like old pennies
they can't be bothered to count.
Fools.
The words are my makeshift wings,

and you may say I cannot fly;
much more bumblebee than fairy
but thirty years these words
have carried me when my legs would not,
comforted me in the cold, biting dark,
warmed me when my too thin spirit
felt the goose-stepping on my grave.

I may not soar with the falcon
riding the thermals in the notch,
I may not glide with willowed grace,
but I do fly, make no mistake.

Now go argue aerodynamics
with a hummingbird,
or lecture the dancing stars
about how their waltz
is simply a trick of light,
or maybe explain to pounding surf
that it won't always be a sea . . .
Me, I'll be gathering the pennies
you dropped in your haste,
and taking a late afternoon fly-by
because the words do it for me.
You can curse your lack of wings,
but that isn't what gives me flight.

ANGEL'S HAIR

Held now in her hand,
cut and neatly bound in a pigtail . . .

Chin length once, that perfect silk
I loved to brush,
perfectly framing that sweet face,
those lovely gray eyes
flecked with amber and green.

Her gift was not for the Magi,
but for someone she had never met,

and she said,
"Maybe it will make them feel better, Momma."

What was the tiny tug at my heart,
mourning those pretty strands,
compared to a small heart
that had already learned
to love beyond her little world?

❧ PINKED

I needed to be out in the same spring breeze
that lifted the skirt of every tree with petals,
so I could brush off the ashes and cobwebs,
blow loose a few lost dreams
and learn to breathe as if
my ribs were not broken again.

Away I went, two-wheeling . . .
dogwood, forsythia, stubborn azaleas,
it felt good to watch the ground
vanish beneath the spinning wheels,
felt grand with a wind on my back.

I had to pause under that tree,
alive with pink flowers
smelling like some rare spice, while
a rascal wind tugged hard the branches
till I was standing in the snow
of pink petals . . . lips, eyes, hair
all gloriously confettied.

And then dear one,
I saw your smile in my mind's eye . . .
this too old flower child
dressed again in petals,
laughing,
waiting for the second
you realized that you simply
had to kiss me again.

❧ Dark Mocha Man

He was the shade of mocha,
with a little less *au lait*,
his eyes the rheumy red
of one who knew too many demon nights,
he stood there managing dignity
as he lined up the Colt 45 quarts,
then looked at mini bottles,
considering his options.

"I like vodka,
but it makes me mean,
so how about two of the rum,
and two Jim Beams.
Cheaper to buy the big ones,
but when they're done, so am I."

I wondered what price he paid,
the Dark Mocha man,
for that bit of wisdom.
I met his eye for just a moment,
his smile was every lost dream,
and he whispered,
"Girl, you don't really wanna know."

❧ Never An Angel

I do not inspire the lighter emotions,
words draped in pastel wash
to raise the eyes to heaven,
and no one will ever call me "angel" . . .
Not with a straight face.

I have no wings,
nor clarion cries to summon chivalry . . .
I am but a woman, mortal,

and I meet your eye,
not seeking the higher plane.

I am never the angel,
never a being of white light,
raising her voice to match the seraphim,
too earthy for cherubim,
and too gentle to hold forth a host,
from the army of heaven.

No.
I am not an angel.
But I am, in more ways than I wish,
your ephemeral.
And you must decide
how much of a lesser soul
you can abide,
before next you hold me,
and take me to a place
we both know
no angel would ever go.

✼ First Ghost

He wrote a poem about her,
a child with huge brown eyes,
who fell to fire. He had taken her,
for I saw her tears in his eyes.

He couldn't leave her to haunt
the jungle leaves, and the short time
it took to cover the small form
became the links in Marley's chain.
When he left, she followed his steps.

She never spoke to him, but as he sat
still in the dark, she would crawl
onto his lap, silent for a while; the first
ghost of a life that left shades in its wake.

"You don't take a man's life,
and not someday know you did,"
he said. But he never said what
happened when things went awry,
or why a rose was staining a small white dress.

❧ PIER GLASS

No mirror can capture the essence
of a spirit that is silvered to purpose.
I am the mercury pressed to glass,
the light inside me
is only the back-flash of visions.
The essence is there
but your fingertips will find only the smooth
because you must live the glass
to know its imperfections,
to see the mottle where the silver thinned,
the bonfire of my own vanity
fed from small wood,
to a blue-hued blaze
where the salamanders dance at will.
The question in the mirror
is always the same . . .
will the flash ever be my own,
or just the reflection
of the constellations that gleam
in the soft shades of nether night?

❧ BUNNY SLIPPERS

I can imagine your outrage,
so male, so butch, so very masculine
if I told you that you are *bunny slippers* to me.
I slip into you with a sigh.
You are warm and comfortable.

It seems you read me
like a Braille rainbow,
arching across all the *me* there is,
making me taste the colors,
creating a spectrum never before seen.
There is no word for that,
no couplet,
no verse . . .
But oh, my dear despite the lick of flame,
despite the hungry eyes
that eat you in small bites,
despite the longing you fuel,
you are the bunny slippers
I never knew,
and I relish the way
you slip into my life,
and wear my heartstrings
to carry your personal totem.

While that may not be the all of it,
still I can say *bunny slippers*
and slip into you
with perfect ease.

ଔ Not So Strong As That

I know you admire me standing . . .
devil may care, ready for anything
but not today please.
Not today.
This moment, this instant
I am more paper mâché than me,
more tinder than tender.
I am so scraped down bleeding,
that one spark will be my Viking funeral.
Emptied of earth,
rickety, run down
I just want to sleep

beyond my dreams.
Much good they do me,
when it hurts to walk.
There is a shiny, silver chair
spinning behind my eyes
and they say the little mermaid could dance,
each step a tread on sharp knives.
She did not cry where they could see her,
so neither shall I.
But I am not so strong as all that
when I feel the wolves start to circle again.
I wonder how long it will be
before my bones are bleaching white this beach.

○§ SMALL MATTER OF TRANSLATION

When a man who tastes
so much like a loved one
looks in your eyes and says
I am not in love with you,
it is wise not to hear "but,"
even if there is one,
most especially if there is not.
I am not in love with you
also means I never will be,
so hoping for such
is simply futile, sad,
and more than a bit daft.
Accept what is said,
do not embellish,
if you still find their arms,
know that love is not included,
nor even an option,
there is no other possible interpretation.
But then . . .
it might just be a small matter of translation.

❧ You Could Miss It

The smile might fool you,
failing that, the laugh
hand on hip, cocksure
so long as you don't look too close.
Mae West is alive and well.

But days like this
I am not hurting anywhere I could name,
still . . . an ache.
Arms more numb than real,
is there really skin on me?

Tonight the moon will shine
tumescent, round and lush.
All I will feel is the fall of silver
to flesh not quite my own.

Not a day for tears or sighs,
just one to remind me
that the deepest part,
the places unseen,
the unwanted end
is always curled inside
waiting to bloom beneath
the next lonesome moon.

But you could miss that.

❧ Inflection Of Silence

Words carry their own sound,
bolts, bangs or bells
striking the heart like a gong.
Even the low, steady beat
carries its own meter,
but there is nothing to equal
the inflection of silence,

the fall of the last "e"
in a word as hard as *please*
torn from a spirit without hope
of return or succor.
Soft as it may seem
there is no harsher tone
then the inflection of silence
where even one word
would be deliverance.

☙ Momma And The Baby Buddha

The first time she sat in my garden,
bathed in sunlight
gurgling,
she held up a chubby fist,
spread the fingers like a lily
and became utterly still.
A honeybee landed on her,
smack in the middle of her hand
and I jumped,
but she just watched
and wondered
until it flew off.

I saw it then,
in falling beams of light,
something behind her eyes
so much wiser than I.
She looked up at me,
and her smile was so gentle,
I did a double-take.
Amused.
I'm fine momma, the look said.
And you'll be fine too.
We have a lot to teach each other;
today we started the lesson
with a honeybee.

I sat beside her,
very quiet,
and knew I was not the one
who would always be doing the teaching.

❦ JUST ANOTHER WAVE

I didn't see it coming either,
it missed me
but you went flying
ass over tea-kettle,
splayed on the sand
grit making raw your knees,
spitting, sputtering,
suddenly winded and wounded
wary and gun shy
wondering how to rise.

I could offer my hand
. . . and do,
reminding you that
your hand was all I ever held.

Now your eyes
are on the Sea,
the same color as mine,
with nothing as certain as you wished.

Easy for me to stand back a little
wax philosophical
and say, "It was just another wave,
you've ridden them before."
Only you know the dark eddies
where you swam alone,
the wrecks beneath the swells
that batter your heart.

I will sit by the shoreline,
watch the pipers and plovers,
and be here to offer a hand

when the next wave
sweeps you fast,
into my cove.

☙ ROOTS AND SHOOTS

The city carves its own markings
on skin or soul or lives,
on sandstone, marble or granite rock
with never the same glyph twice,
but the carvings stay,
weathering near to fade
visible only to those
who wear the same mark.

It should not surprise you
that I see the world at times
from your own peculiar angle,
though I am a woman,
and not from your streets.
I remember my own.

I remember the fruit peddler,
who drove the open truck
bananas, apples, grapes . . .
driving slow, up and down the street,
calling his wares in that voice and tone:

Ayyyyy bananas . . . apples . . .
oranges . . . five for a buck
getcher bananas here.

I remember the blacktop park
where the kids broke bottles
brown, green and clear
the moonlight on the right night
made the place glitter,
maybe it was not paradise,
but it was where my roots began.
I wonder my friend

what city whimsy
you carried to the shoots
of your grown up dreams?

ଓଃ Rappin Rapunzel

Hey there prince,
you think you're fine,
laying down love,
quite nearly divine,
so while you're looking
at my braid,
ready to swing,
hey, I'm not the maid.

(Ppppttttt pppptttt pttttt)

You say you wanna save me,
now ain't that sweet?
But you look a little pudgy
kinda wide in the seat,
and since it's my hair that's hangin,
I'm sorry to say
you'll just have to find
a less painful way!

(Pppppppttt pppttttt pttttt)

Well I'm not brilliant,
but it seems to me,
a ladder would work wonders
for getting me free,
so go to the village
on your trusty steed,
I'm sure Cottage Depot
will have what you need.

(Pttttt ptttttt ptttttt)

And when I am loose,
I'll give you a chance,

you can show me your place,
and maybe your lance
but as long as I'm stuck
in this tower so high,
you're not climbing my hair,
and coming up dry.

I'm Rappin Rapunzel, Rappin Rapunzel . . .

❧ Maybe Snow

They say we will have snow,
a dusting to frost the hills.
And something inside of me
goes into winter mode,
something else goes to you,
wide-eyed, tender
remembering that in the cold
we began with a kiss on the wrist,
those *you could almost taste me* eyes,
so silly and sentimental in a sweater.

I think of you when night falls quick,
the small chill from my window
makes me wish for the jazz cafe,
the dance, and the smile
that says only one woman
knows the winter witchery
to melt the frost from your night,
gives you small delight
to the soft lick of piano keys
when a touch said enough to us both.

❧ Plan B

Plan A is simple, really.
But everything I am
is riding on one pass of the dice,
while I stand buck naked in the Casino
trying not to remember
that every time I gamble, I lose.

Focus girl.
Get into the words . . .
tell the story, you know you can,
and pray the dice are not loaded,
because plan B sucks.
Plan B is to go quietly insane,
die inside . . .
become a smiling husk,
days too long to bother counting.
The words die too,
since it will not matter
if even I don't care to hear them.

Plan B is taking the pills
they say will make this life
easier to tolerate,
because after all, honey,
no one has it good
and maybe it's all just a blink
between baby carriage
and funeral cars.
But anti-depressants
are for people who don't know why
. . . and I do.
This is not an *inappropriate reaction*,
this is all out war against something
that stopped working long ago.
I can haul myself out,
or I can just give it up.

This time, there is no plan B.

☙ Got Wood?

There are ways to make a fire,
that will last both day and night . . .
but you have to treat the wood
special if you want it to burn slow,
and give off the light and heat
just so . . .

I will start with tinder,
small touches and curls,
set up the kindling
so that when I strike the match
everything is ready
to *catch*.

Actually,
you don't have to
stroke the wood,
to stoke the flame,
but the oils from skin
never hurt a stout log,
so you won't mind
if I go with the grain?

And now I am ready.
Do me a favor, will you?
Give me that wood *now* . . .
and don't worry about fancy
because sometimes
you just can't beat
honest, white heat . . .

❧ Vernal

Spring cannot dance,
nor bud, nor bloom
there can be no ballet
without the hard frost
that grays the day
or aches in the bones.

One season must give way
for another to pass,
the bleak chill setting the stage
for delicate tracery,
the warm to come.

Do not count the days
as if the seasons
are dressed in regret,
or you will not feel
the warmth,
the sweet seduction
the green velvet of Spring
when next she leaps
to the place where only winter stood.

❧ Tangible 24

There is a pattern to the need,
a place where the playful falls away,
the skin seems peeled back,
baring every nerve end
to the possibility of your touch.
One day given to the moon,
where calm thought is impossible,
and I become the virgin
possessed by a ravening spirit
that hungers for flesh
to join me in reveling.

That one day in each 30
I keep to myself,
wear modest clothing
and do not meet the eyes of any,
because that day I am consumed,
lust is too pretty a word
for the pulsing between these thighs.
Oh god,
the weight of cloth to skin
is an unbearable friction.

What your hands
or your tongue,
or your rampant flesh
would feel like against this new skin
is a matter of sweet torment.
I want to sink before you,
desperate, supplicant
and flaunt the honey
that wets my walk,
fall open as every bit of blood
floods my lips,
plumping them for the taking,
priming them for your thrust,
preparing me
for the feel of you
when I am so far beyond consent.

Take me roughly,
hand wound tight in my hair,
pound deeply in
where the flesh gapes,
or take the darker fruit
or fill my mouth
with your flesh
so that my only sound
is a muffled moan
breathed joyously
against veins throbbing,
pulsing need

fed by this wild hunger
that makes me shake.

No time for love making,
no time for pretty,
and do not tease . . . *Take!*
Not once . . .
once cannot fill,
not twice . . .
but over and over till
this tense 24
has passed again
leaving me full,
sated
and able to be
the calm playful lover you know
when the moon does not possess my soul,
or demand sexual sacrifice
as the desired coin
to redeem my skin.

ଔ The Heart Of Me

I watch it flow, twitch, flutter,
black and white imagery
taken through skin . . .
my daughter's heart beating.

I remember
when first I saw her
curled inside me,
so tiny
with one wild pulse
to mark her center.

And fourteen years later,
I am watching again,
wondering what this pulse
or that hitch means.

I try not to make her laugh . . .
but that's what I do
when I am scared.
Crack jokes to show the gods
my mortal valor.

"Go haunt another life,
where they fear you," I say.
"But leave me and mine be!"

Such brittle bravado
as I watch
my daughters beating heart.

❧ CRUNCHING NUMBERS

A life spent apprenticed to math,
applied sciences and logical sequence
leaves little room for the factor X,
when it is more than unknown,
when it is something felt by senses
outside the brackets,
but too sure to be random numbers.

Do the math if you must,
but all the neatly scripted exponents
will never give more than theory
to the inexact science of being . . .
never explain who you are,
or why,
and cannot even begin
to fill in the blanks of *us*.

I lived without the symmetry
of the math-ruled life,
but now need the comfort
of something not left to metaphysics
kismet, or the unknowable will
of an older deity with an odd sense of humor.

We should not be parts of the same equation,
not even the same page of notation,
yet there is no denying strange attraction,
or the way the numbers slide away
when I am X,
and you are Why.

❧ MODERN DAY LADY GODIVA

I know that *nice* women
didn't do such things in their day,
and she had both daring
and compassion on her side,
but today?
A beautiful celebrity
rides a horse naked?
No courage in that really.
Just a photo op for Papparazi,
the cover of *People*,
and maybe ten minutes
of water cooler chat.

No.
Brave would be a woman of *my* years,
hoisting skin no longer fresh,
lined with seams and scars
to the back of a horse,
knowing I would not be beautiful,
just . . . *naked.*

Harder to face the eyes of those
who would rather I stumbled
from middle age to golden years
decently covered,
than to expose myself to their gaze.

Maybe this is how
I'll celebrate fifty . . .
"Jesus, lady,

cover it up for God's sake."
And if I am half
of who I hope to be,
perhaps I will smile serenely
as they haul away
the Modern Day Lady Godiva.

ଔ THE KIDS IN THE BACK ROW

It was a soft event,
folk music . . .
Keelaghan? Williams?
No matter.
The singer was stroking a love song
as if it were the only woman
he ever loved,
and the sigh was universal.
I looked around,
and there they were . . . *Again.*
Shameless.
She was leaning back in her man's arms
and his lips were warm to her throat.
They were floating on that song,
and you couldn't miss the yin and yang of them.
I looked away . . .
pure envy because the *kids* in the back
were 62 and 70 years old.
Their faces told me
that love has no time limit.
These two had found each other
and that meant . . . maybe . . .
someday . . . maybe,
I could be
a grown up kid
nuzzled in the back row,
long past the day
when necking was deemed improper.

❧ Not My Buddha

You are a nasty bit of work,
for all that you wear,
the saffron robes of enlightenment,
chant the money hum,
claim to own
constant cosmic truth;
when now and again
you trifle with zen
as if you knew karma
like nobody's business.

But Buddha is serene, bub,
and I haven't seen anything from you
that smacks of bliss,
just face slaps
you offer as alleged wake-up calls
from the Universe.
So let's just get this clear
here and now, *little man* . . .
maybe you can peddle
your wax flowers as real
to someone who needs illusions
more than truth,
but you ain't my Buddha, buddy.
The door's that way.

❧ Vintage

There are wines to tease the tongue,
heady vapors to enthrall
amusing little pressings
but I like best of all

the wine no one expected
to be a vintage pick,

when it delivers extra pleasure
not just a Bacchus kick.

There are Beaujolais, and Rieslings,
Merlot, and Pinot Fine,
but I look for more than just the grape
when I am choosing wine.

I look for something lesser known,
with a label not so clever,
for the proof of any vintage
will own another measure.

The sparkling wines of yesterday,
were voguish in their day,
but I will savor the richer flavor
because it has more to say.

You seem to be a better choice,
to go with beef or fish . . .
with all the sweetness I could crave,
you offer all I wish.

So do not fear the newer wines,
that some might care to crow,
you'll always be my vintage dear,
I thought that you should know.

ᏩᏃ Brunch Date

Where the hell is my blouse?
Heels?
Omigod! This looks like
I beat up a bag lady for it . . .
eyes to the clock . . . *ten minutes?*

Living room looks like an insurance ad
about natural disaster.
The coddled eggs are closer to curdled.
The orange juice for the mimosas
is puddling on my kitchen floor

and the muffins are ready
because the smoke detector
just went off . . .

I simply will not discuss hair,
Okay . . .
I'll do the makeup thing . . .
Owwwww, Mascara in the eye
which now is red and teary . . .

and this seemed like such a good idea,
a leisurely brunch for two,
reading the Sunday paper together
to show you I was capable
of a conversation,
insights,
and a sentence that did not include
"take me before I die,"
or other incoherencies.

The doorbell?
God, please kill me this instant.

Oh . . . Hi.
Sorry the place is...
what do you mean *comfortable*?
The meal is a bit of a...
What's that?
A picnic hamper?
You brought brunch?
Well I'll just go get present...
oh . . .
mmmmmmm . . .
ahh . . . omigod . . .
Beautiful? Me?

"That's it sir.
Right here, right now,
oh god,
take me before I die."
We'll talk about the economy over dinner.

• 175 •

❦ ANGEL BORN

I hated the belly touching
that most seemed to think
was neat and expected
when I began to show . . .
slapped away hands
that seemed to touch
not only my body,
but you.

Then one day
five weeks before you were expected
I found myself in the market
choosing tomatoes and cukes for salad
and when I turned,
a man stood there . . .
thin, elderly
but his face lit
by the most astounding smile.
Before I could breathe,
he reached out both hands
and touched my belly.

"Beautiful," he whispered.
I looked at his face,
saw it light with something,
and I would have moved away,
back . . .
and then I saw it.
Blue numbers faded
on a thin forearm
the skin-like crepe paper.

You were dreaming
as you often did
sleeping inside me.
You had moved twice
just twice in all those months.
But as I stood there,

with a strange, sweet man
touching my belly
you moved once again.

He felt it and began to cry.
"Beautiful," he whispered, "beautiful."
In that instant
I felt the tiny wet
and all unknowing,
you began your swim
from me to this world.

He stepped back
and spoke softly to his wife,
who then tried to explain
that he didn't know much English,
had never done such a thing . . .

I looked into his amazing blue eyes,
shining with tears of wonder,
looked at the blue mark on his arm,
reached out,
took his hand
and laid it again, gently on my belly.
"Beautiful," I said, nodding.

Two days later, sweet angel girl,
they showed you to me,
21 inches long,
6 pounds, 13 ounces, five weeks premature,
but perfect.
He had been right,
that man who's name I never knew.
You were beautiful.
and always will be.

Your birth gave me joy . . .
but my sweet child,
you also gave back hope,
and something else lost
to a man who had known
the death of dreams.

I saw in his eyes
the miracle that you would be.
The world is lighter
because you came into it.

⌘ Children's Hospital

Pretty murals,
floors buffed to high gloss,
the quiet you associate
with perhaps a library.

Registration,
same questions:
name
address
age
insurance?

My eyes are drawn
to the parents.
Our children sit and play
while we are left to prove
that they are worthy,
eligible for the attention.

Not one seems to belong here,
save they are getting "the look"
I see in my daughters eyes.

Too many doctors
have asked too many questions,
even though she does not hurt.
She asks me with her eyes
for a nanosecond
the question I cannot answer.

Mom, why am I here?
She is not afraid yet,
but she knows there is no medicine for this.

I am fighting for a way
to explain that she is fine,
wonderful,
bright,
beautiful,
and that this thing
makes her no different,
no less special to her momma's heart.

I see the eyes of the other moms
the other dads
and I know that their children
are like mine.
No one is here for an allergy shot,
or a booster.
They don't send you here
for those simple things.

We lock eyes and nod,
try to smile and seem like we are not praying
for the souls we too dearly love
in the lobby of St. Christopher's Hospital.

I'm grateful for the colors,
for the neat decor,
for the gentle folks who love my kid.
But God,
I never wanted to see this place.

ᘓ Gazing At Goya
(Another Part)

I saw it in her eyes,
languid, lusty,
almost amused
as her lover toiled
to capture her flesh,
sweating as the light faded,
knowing he counted the seconds

till he could cast down palette and brush,
and touch her
with his own pigments,
his own colors,
knowing that *not quite* smile
hid a rage of feminine heat,
wanting to take her mouth
and change the gentle sweet tease
into something
that would fuel his brush
when next the light
blessed her flesh.

ᛯ Midnight Embers

I find myself pulling you close,
wrapping myself around the memory
of you and your touch,
knowing that tonight,
this is as close as we might get.

Bittersweet . . . the tang of honey and lemon
but soothing still.
I need this time alone
to remind myself
that I can be without you,
those sweet words
that addictive touch.

And just when I think I'm fine,
five sorts of noble,
my mind strays back to you again.
Wondering,
worrying like a bad tooth,
that I touch with my tongue
knowing it can hurt me,
but not able to resist.

You're fine, I tell myself.
I'm just peachy
so why are you
the drug I crave,
the ghost of a taste to my heart
and why when I escape to sleep
do I find you waiting for me
if I really didn't need you tonight?

ℜ Reaching For White

The sun rose on fields
snow-blown and misted
with ghostly swirls and dervishes.
No fog, this . . .
for fog simply lies.

This was living
as it arched and twisted,
fingering out to the road
and reaching for me
like the shade of a beloved friend.

There was white inside,
trying to seep out of pores,
and I felt it strain
trying to mesh and meld
with this sentient wraith
fingers touching
joining
and suddenly
I am the morning mist
dancing in the crystal air.

⌘ THE MAN THAT IS, THE BOY THAT WAS

A life
speaks plainly of itself,
breathing, sharing, exposing . . .
yet the Gordian knot
of the spirit within
remains untouched,
not known, perhaps never knowable.

There are softly spoken hints
that echo to the ear,
wry truth offered
by a soul too long viewing
a funhouse mirror
and thinking it is real.

But even if my eyes witness
an updated image of skin,
what I *feel* is a boy
with a buzz-cut, running
full-out across a grass field,
who wants to shout
the truth of himself
to an eye-watering summer sky;

A boy who wraps himself
in a cocoon of someday
eyes bright with wishes, promises
and the blaze of every shooting star
deep inside the boy that is,
awaiting the man
he will someday be.

❧ Simple Sipping

Morning caught,
a thousand details to a day,
and somewhere between forgotten things
and the things I can not forget
you are there in cashmere
maybe rugged-handsome in Nautica,
with a mug of morning brew
just like the one I hold.
It looks like *sipping* you do,
just the trace of a taste,
but I can see the wheels turning
and you don't miss much
with those eyes that take it all in,
do the math of a life
and still wonder at the spark.
What you don't get right
you fake nicely,
and the confident air
you give off like breathing
keeps the unwary barbarians
rocking on the balls of their feet.
They may not see what I do,
but you prefer it that way.
Better they not guess
that the quiet one
walks with big brass,
acquired with wit and skill.
Better they not suspect
the man beneath the smile.
I blunder through days unplanned,
my morning brew sweet and hot,
wondering how you came to be
in the process of simple sipping
so much the way
I like to take my coffee.

❧ Writing Around The Cliché

Cartwheels and splits,
handsprings and double-dervish stunts
anything to avoid penning
that cliché you don't need.

But we know each other too well
I thought if I did not speak it
if I denied it the letters,
it would fade to thin.

But the damned emotion
burrowed into every move I make,
tiny tendrils reaching to you
no matter that I am not trying.

I told myself your logic would
dull the cutting,
told myself you would not feel
the razor of *separate*,
even whispered alone in the dark
that you never did need me.

Then I saw your face,
your eyes
the way you seemed to sink
so comfortably into my arms.
It was blunt, and simple.
I will not say what you do not,
but that doesn't make it
less true,
not for you or me.

No matter that I contort the words,
no matter that I bite my tongue
and write around the edge
of the daydreams and night ventures.
I am still reaching for you
and I long for that cliché
that we do not speak.

❧ Binaries

It's all one's and zero's, you know . . .
coded, and suddenly a door opened.
All at once I understood the blatant
Oh sailor, I love you soooo good,
or *hey, wanna cyber?*
and all the other fan dancing
posturing, pretending;
all the nonsense that repelled me
and made this place
something I mostly hid in.

It's about binaries . . .
and if the only values
are one or zero
then you damned well better be a *one*
because *zero* will always be nothing.

So they will be anything you'd like,
fearing they are not enough.
And that may work for some;
but me?
I never was . . . a number.

❧ The Rules Of Riptide

"The shortest distance between two points..."
until you toss in a curve ball.

Swim for shore when the riptide has you,
and the sea is a demon
wrapped around your ankles,
with the sand so close
every stroke to it hauls you back
your body clings to the logic
that straight is best,

and your heart pounds within you,
till panic finds its footing.

You have to swim with the riptide
parallel to shore,
force yourself not to look
at where you want so much to be,
because any moment you will bolt,
and if it does not let you go,
you will die
doing what seemed safest
and most sane.

☙ This Woman

This woman is not the Frazetta ideal;
voluptuous body bound in metal and leather,
with legs that never end;
bitch goddess to the elements.

This woman is soft to the touch,
ripe to the taste,
and spiced with a thousand dreams
she will never speak of,
even to you who made her dream.

This woman has breasts
that harden to aching
from your look;
turn to honey
from the lightest touch.

This woman is soft flesh
wrapped around a soul
that gives as good as it gets.

This woman will not kneel
but will offer herself
with the quiet dignity
of one called queen,

earth mother,
soul seeker,
lover;

a woman content in her skin.

◆ His Bohemian

You can almost glimpse
the light of Romany fires
in the flash of her eyes,
flesh cameo pale,
mouth soft like a kiss asked
from a woman too shy to say
how she longs to touch you.

His bohemian,
poetry in her blood,
like the high peal of gypsy violin,
lover from a time
when the name held
something of honor.

His bohemian,
scented with pollen
he never breathed,
his passionate woman
giving a name to longing,
and warmth to a winter eve;
her voice half laughter,
someone he may never own,
but somehow always has.

❧ KNOWLEDGE AND KNOWING

Something known is never unlearned,
even when it is forgotten,
or simply half remembered.
We can never learn enough to erase
something else we discovered
by chance or happenstance,
or even when the knowledge
was offered with innocent intent.

Always, there is the knowing unspoken,
a hundred years of elements
will still yield rubbings revealed
to soft carbon, and patience.
Youth demands to know all,
taste all, be all things.
I am not so old that I have no taste
for wonder, or adventure.
I am just old enough to understand
that such will always carry a price,
and now I am imbued with knowledge
waiting calmly
to see what will come
of this moment rich with the tactile.

Lips can never be un-kissed.
Skin can never be un-caressed.
A heart can never be unhandled,
and I cannot forget
a single moment of knowing.

Lisa Shields
February 2005

Autobiography

I was born (the youngest of four children) in 1960, in Jersey City. New Jersey has been my home for most of my life.

My first attempts at poetry emerged when I was in 7th grade. Words fascinated me and poetry became my "niche."

While in college, I received the Ester Bovard Medallion for excellence in creative writing.

I married Charles Shields in 1987. In 1991, I was blessed with the birth of my daughter, Desiree Angelique.

The constants in my life have been poetry and a passionate desire to be a positive influence.

I have learned that even under the worst of circumstances, the human spirit soars in search of hope, truth and love. If that sounds overly romantic, I make no apology.

Thank you, my reader, for welcoming a part of my world into yours. May you know kindness, fortune and love for all of your days, and may you always be touched by the infinite charm of firefly glow.

Lisa Shields

www.ingramcontent.com/pod-product-compliance
Lightning Source LLC
Chambersburg PA
CBHW071705090426
42738CB00009B/1674